Praise for Alicia Forest and her work...
(from people just like you...)

For her complimentary online newsletter...

"I look forward to Alicia's newsletter each week since it always contains clear, actionable suggestions to increase the revenues in my business. Abundance is about more than money, and Alicia demonstrates that in her positive mental attitude and focus on having a great life, not just making a great living."

Pamela Slim
Author, *Escape from Cubicle Nation: From Corporate Prisoner to Thriving Entrepreneur*
Author, *Body of Work*
escapefromcubiclenation.com

"Alicia, when I first started out looking for information about online marketing, I signed up for about a dozen newsletters. What I found is that even among the 'big boys,' yours is the most user-friendly and comprehensive out there. I've applied more of your tips than I can count and because of that I now have a fantastic 'free taste,' my first e-book is selling great and I have a growing list of warm prospects who receive my newsletter. Thank you, Alicia!"

Elizabeth Chamberlain
space-lift.com

"Alicia, the tips and articles you offer in your newsletter have proven to increase my success and productivity time and time again. They are so simple and easy to implement! Thank you, it's just what I need!"

Sandra De Freitas
Author, *Does This Blogsite Make My Wallet Look Fat?*
wpblogsites.com

"I look forward to your ezine every week! I love the practical, real advice!"

Laura West
joyfulbusiness.com

"Your newsletter is one of my favourite newsletters, and I regularly take the time to read and digest the information. I love the personality you put into it, especially updating us about Chloe and Jack. I have a folder which I keep your newsletters in, so that I don't 'accidentally' delete them!"

Tracey Lawton
traceylawton.com

"Your newsletter is always warm and friendly with the added bonus of having much useful information. Your articles are thought-provoking and inspire many great ideas. I look forward to receiving it!"

Felicia J. Slattery, M.A., M.Ad.Ed.
CommunicationTransformation.com

"Alicia, your newsletter is always a welcome event - I read it right away, bookmark it for great ideas, and always file it so I can refer to it time and time again. Great job! Please keep up the great work!"

Mary McDonald, CEO
mcdcg.com

"I consider your newsletter as one of the top marketing newsletters that I consistently read."

Robert Lowe
RSL Marketing

"Most of my email is a burden… not interesting, not requested… I welcome Alicia's newsletter! She always has valuable information included and I love the personal touch of talking about her family."

Suzanne Holman, MAEd
suzanneholman.com

"I look forward to reading your newsletter every Sunday. Each article is short, concise and valuable. Alicia is an outstanding educator and I've watched my business grow in a very short time thanks to her wise advice."

Katyayani Poole, Ph.D.
SanskritforYogis.com

Get your complimentary subscription at:
http://aliciaforest.com

6 SIMPLE STEPS

to 6 Figures
for the
SOLO SERVICE PROFESSIONAL

How to Create Your Lifestyle Business
Based on Your Passion for Serving Others

Alicia Forest, MBA

**6 SIMPLE STEPS TO 6 FIGURES FOR THE
SOLO SERVICE PROFESSIONAL
HOW TO CREATE YOUR LIFESTYLE BUSINESS BASED
ON YOUR PASSION FOR SERVING OTHERS**

iUniverse books may be ordered through booksellers or by contacting:

iUniverse
1663 Liberty Drive
Bloomington, IN 47403
www.iuniverse.com
1-800-Authors (1-800-288-4677)

ISBN: 978-0-5954-3014-7 (sc)
ISBN: 978-1-4401-7346-2 (hc)
ISBN: 978-0-5958-7355-5 (e)

Printed in the United States of America.

iUniverse rev. date: 07/17/2014

Dedication

To my husband James ~ for your unwavering
love, support and belief in me…
gratitude is a tiny word

CONTENTS

ACKNOWLEDGMENTS

Today is where your book begins
The rest is still unwritten...
- 'Unwritten' by Natasha Bedringfield

It starts with a whisper, a quiet visit to your thoughts, the slightest tug to your heart. In moments of silence, you can almost hear a gentle song in the wind. Something is calling you. Something is seeking you. Something is waiting for you.

It's your purpose. Your passion. Your reason for being. Whether it's meant for only a moment or a lifetime, it's waiting for you to claim it. You have the choice to ignore it, to focus your energy and thoughts elsewhere, but it's always going to be waiting for you to embrace it.

I've spent my whole life trying to hear it, trying to embrace it, trying to reach it, but always failing, sometimes feeling so close, but still managing to turn in another direction all the same.

That is, until now. It never went away. It still whispered to me, at night when the world was still but my mind was not. It visited my thoughts during those rare quiet times I allowed myself. It tugged at my heart almost daily.

And then I started to talk. And I realized that what I'd been doing all this time was trying to get back to me, to the person I was before (and the before is much too long of a story for this book). I couldn't move forward until I realized that there was a 'me' that existed before. It sounds so simple, really. But to me it was a revelation. Knowing she existed and that I could get back to her opened my ears, my mind and my heart. I could embrace it – that which was seeking me...

And I understood that the question wasn't so much why was I so often not the person I wanted to be, but why was I so often not the person I am? Once I really got that, everything changed... in my life and with my business.

This book is the result.

It is with bottomless gratitude that I thank all of my guides, my whisperers, on this path...

To my mom and dad for the lessons they taught me about strength and resilience, and for passing along the entrepreneurial blood.

To Tony Robbins for introducing me to the concept of coaching at the very beginning.

To the late Steve Smith (aka Hurricane) for re-introducing me to Tony's materials and my passion for them ten years later.

To Chris Barrow for that moment at the end of his event that solidified my commitment to becoming a coach and for introducing me to Andrea Lee.

To Andrea Lee for putting your message out there in the world in a way that I could hear it, for the MSOCI/MSCC/Lab membership, and for the transformational opportunity to be your client, and join your team as a multiple streams licensed coach, and so very much more.

To Kendall SummerHawk for the incredible and life-altering experience of working with you one-on-one. We ended up in so much more of an amazing place than I ever imagined.

To Sandra De Freitas – I couldn't ask for a better BBF…

To my clients for their enthusiasm and support for me and each other – you continue to inspire me to do what I do… and I love you for it!

To my virtual team – I simply couldn't do it without you.

To Dr. Raskin for leading me so gently and patiently back to me…

To my husband James for his utter belief in my ability to do anything and be really successful at it. And to my daughter Chloe and my son Jack for being my biggest and littlest motivators and inspirers.

I've finally heard the whisper. Today is where my book begins…

AUTHOR'S NOTE

Once upon a time...

I had a marketing/public relations/web development business that I started for one main reason, which just might sound familiar to you...

I wanted to be my own boss, have the option to make as much money as I wanted, and have control over my life. I'd had countless jobs, all of which I was very good and very successful at, but I really struggled with working for someone else. I hated having to ask permission to take time off, and inwardly I constantly battled with the prevailing mindset that the job was more important than anything else. But I figured I just had to earn my wings, and once I did that, I'd be a lot happier working for someone else.

At the age of 29, I was head of the public relations and marketing department of a private university. I was one of only a handful of senior staff members who had decision-making powers and who counseled the university president. I was also the spokesperson for the college, meaning I dealt with the media in good times and in bad. It was a heady position for someone so young.

I held that position for over two years, and I was as happy as I could have been in it. I very much enjoyed the collegiate environment; my boss, the university president, was the best one I'd ever had. My salary was double my age, which was a big marker of success at the time. I could work from home when I wanted, I had wonderful assistants, and I could take time off without too much hassle.

And still, I was miserable.

So, on January 2, 2001, I worked out a deal and left the university with both fear and excitement thudding in my heart. It was the best decision I've ever made and I've never looked back.

I launched my marketing/ public relations/web development business (I had also been in charge of the university's website so I had learned a lot about web technology) with exactly <u>one</u> client. And I did all the traditional things that everyone tells you to do - I joined the local chamber of commerce and attended countless networking breakfasts. I sent direct mail, trying to drum up business. I even cold-called for about a week to see what happened.

And what happened? I struggled and struggled to get clients. I was trading my time for money and I was getting nowhere fast. At the time, I was in the middle of a divorce, and I was constantly worried about paying my bills. There came a time when I thought I was going to have to close my business and go back to work for someone else.

But I was determined NOT to let that happen - ever.

So I immersed myself in learning from other very successful entrepreneurs who'd already figured out how to make it work. I invested in myself and my business by hiring my own coach, and as soon as I started implementing the strategies and tactics I learned from my coach and other mentors, things started to turn around in my business.

Since then I've tested out many strategies and various models, and found what worked extremely well for me. That's when I moved into generating multiple 6-figures in my business, with far less effort and much more joy.

All along I was teaching my clients what I learned and more importantly what worked, and they started enjoying their own successes, and I couldn't have been happier. It's how I continue to teach and coach clients today, to even greater success.

It's truly an incredible feeling, to know you're doing what you love to do, with the people you love to do it with, making the kind of income you love to make - and still have a ton of time to really enjoy your life.

Make no mistake - it took me about three years to figure it and then put it into a system that consistently brings me clients, customers and cash (and that was while being pregnant and raising two babies!). But it doesn't have to take you three years or more. In fact, with the information I'm sharing with you in this book, you can go from $0 to consistent cash flow a lot sooner than that. How do I know that? Because I've done it and thousands of my clients have done it too.

What has using this 6-step system I've created brought into my life?

FREEDOM, which is my #1 value. That means I can travel while still easily running my business from wherever I am. For nine summers now, I get to treat my family to spending the entire summer on vacation at the lake where I spent my summers growing up. And, most important to me, I'm able to stay home to raise our two children while still contributing significantly to my family financially. My work allows me the flexibility and the finances to spend both quality and quantity time with Chloe, Jack and James – and nothing means more to me than that.

I'm going to show you exactly how to do this for yourself in this book.

I've invested a lot of time and money into figuring out a system that works - because I had to if I didn't ever want to go back to working for someone else, and if I wanted to continue to work for myself so I could raise my kids.

The system I've developed, based not just on my learning, but on my doing, has helped me to become known as an industry expert, get thousands of visitors to my website who are my ideal customers and clients, convert those visitors into members of my online community via my email list, create and market information products that bring me leveraged income via my website, help more people while making more money, and allow me to enjoy working with a handful of my ideal clients one-on-one. And I do all of this while working less than 15 hours per week.

A constant frustration I've heard over and over from business owners like you is that you don't know what to do or, if you do know, you don't know what order to do things in most effectively and effortlessly, and that you're working too hard for too little return.

With 6 Simple Steps to 6 Figures, you'll get the critical underpinnings and foundation for a truly successful and sustainable business, built on your terms in your time.

Shall we?

INTRODUCTION

If you have built castles in the air, your work need
not be lost; there is where they should be. Now
put foundations under them. ~ Thoreau

KNOW THIS: Creating a profitable online business is as much about marketing as it is about the services, programs and products you offer.

So, before we begin, I want you to take a minute and consider how you think about marketing.

Do you:

- Feel overwhelmed and confused by what to do, how to do it, and/or when to do it?
- Think marketing is just a small part of your business development?
- Think 'marketing = selling' and feel all the negative feelings connected to feeling 'sleazy'?
- Know marketing is something you have to do, but wish you didn't have to?
- Get anxious just thinking about it?

If that's how you think, well, it's time for a serious marketing mindset shift. If you TRULY want to be successful (and I mean, really successful, like having an ABUNDANCE of clients, money, time, freedom, etc.), then you need to change your thinking about what marketing IS and what it isn't.

So let's address each of those negative thoughts now:

1. Marketing is not rocket science – seriously. It is common sense, consistent action, and simple systems. I know you've got the common sense, and I'm giving you a simple and proven system to get you started with this book. All you need to do is make the commitment to take consistent action by following the 6 Steps.

2. Marketing is NOT a small part of your business. Marketing your business is AS important as what it is that you do. You need to make marketing one of your two top priorities of each work day (the other being your work with and for your clients). You must consider marketing as just that important if you want to stay in business and be successful.

3. Marketing is a form of selling AND you can market yourself authentically, I promise. You need to find your own voice (and we'll work on that as we craft your message) and your own story (something else we'll work on), but you can put yourself out there as someone who has gifts to give to the world and feel really, really good about it.

4. My good friend and fellow super-successful entrepreneur, Marney Makridakis (www.artellaland.com), puts it this way: 'There are loads of people out there just waiting for what it is that you have to offer. They need it and want it, and are happy to pay for it. Everyone feels good and everyone wins.' We'll work on marketing yourself ethically and with integrity and you'll never have to feel 'sleazy' about it again.

5. If you keep yourself a secret then no one will know about you. It seems obvious but it's amazing how many solo service professionals think that clients will just show up without them having to do much of anything to make that happen. You must market, but again – it's not hard – especially when you have the tools and resources you need to get you on your way that I'm sharing with you in this book.

6. Put your anxiety aside and have faith. You've made the investment in yourself and in this book. You've taken the first step. Now keep reading, commit to implementing each of the steps, and you will be well on your way to enjoying your own successful and sustainable business!

I hope this helps to shift your mindset around marketing, because now I want to introduce you to the Online Business Breakthrough Formula for creating multiple leveraged streams of income, and the Online Business Breakthrough Marketing & Product Funnel – both of which will make building your business much easier, much more fun, and much more profitable!

Here's the **Online Business Breakthrough Formula:**

Your Unique Message + Your Niche + Your Niche's Problem + Your Solution Package = Your Profitable Product/Program/Service

Just a note here: You don't use the formula just once. You can use it over and over, for as many problems your niche faces, to create as many streams of income as you want. Exciting, isn't it? I'll be talking about the Online Business Breakthrough Formula throughout this book.

You may be familiar with the marketing and product funnel business model. It's the model I followed when I started out and still use today, though modified, to continually meet or to stay ahead of market changes and trends.

To give you a better idea of what I'm talking about, I'd like you to picture a funnel. It's wide at the top and tapers down to a narrow opening, right? Now, when your prospects enter your Funnel through your ezine (online newsletter) or other Free Taste (freebie offering), they are in the 'getting to know you' level of the Funnel. Once they get to know you, like you and trust you, they likely will move down to the next level, which will include your for-fee products and services, your least expensive ones first, increasing in value and cost as they continue downwards, until they eventually get to hiring you one-on-one or to your other big ticket item. That's basically how the funnel system of marketing works.

I see a lot of solo service professionals offer a freebie at the top of their Funnel, and then their one-on-one service packages at the bottom, with nothing in between. But when you offer your products and services at different price points, you are lowering the financial and emotional risk for your prospects by giving them the option to invest in you for free or for a much smaller amount than they would if they were to hire you one-on-one. You are essentially making it impossible for them *not* to buy from you by offering your products and/or services in different packages at different price points.

Using the Formula and the Funnel as our foundation, let's dive deep into each of the Steps now…

THE 6 STEPS

STEP 1

What's Your Unique Message & How Are You Meant to Serve?

You may wonder what your 'unique message' has to do with building your business. It's simple, really…

If you come from an authentic place, success is guaranteed.

Let's set you up for success from the beginning and find that authentic place for you now.

Reminder: Here's the **Online Business Breakthrough Formula:**

Your Unique Message + Your Niche + Your Niche's Problem + Your Solution Packaged = Your Profitable Product/Program/Service

I'm going to share something with you that I usually do in-depth with my private clients. It's called the Center of Authenticity question.

If you're just starting out in your solo service business and need to truly make yourself and your business stand out from the crowd, then answering this question will move you leaps towards that end. If you're already in business for yourself, answering this question will help you define the benefits of your services from a deeper authentic place that will not only make you more memorable, but will draw more of those ideal clients to you as well.

Center of Authenticity question:

'What has happened in your life, good or bad, that would be the most useful to share with others?'

For example, maybe you've gone through a divorce that was difficult and the people in your life seem to remark frequently how well you've handled things. You could create a service business around helping others through the same experience.

Or maybe you're a teacher and you constantly get accolades from parents and colleagues about how well you work with the difficult kids in the classroom. You could create a service business where you work with those kids specifically.

Or perhaps you're a stay-at-home mom who is exceptionally good at living well on a budget. You could create a service business based on your tips and techniques that have worked well for you.

Or maybe you're a yoga instructor, massage therapist, day spa owner, or provide other healing arts services. You can take your experience and knowledge about your industry online to create additional income streams for your business.

In one of marketing expert Seth Godin's books, *All Marketers Are Liars,* he talks about how marketing is really storytelling. Not made-up stories, but authentic stories that help sell a product or service.

Think about your story, your life as it has unfolded up to today, and answer the following additional questions to hone in on your answer to the Center of Authenticity question.

1. How did you get where you are today?
2. What event(s) caused you to be on the path you are on?
3. What reason(s) do you do what you do (or what you want to do)?

If you already have a service business, or if you already know what it is that you want to offer to the world and who you want to offer it to, then you might not feel the need to answer these questions, but I encourage you to do so. Once you have a compelling answer to the Center of Authenticity question and have weaved a story around it that you can share with others, you will be creating a connection with them that simply doesn't come from saying, 'I'm an author and a speaker' or 'I'm a life coach".

Because most likely whatever service you are providing, there was a path that led you to want to do what you do - and people are interested in that. Telling people your story - how you got to where you are and why you are doing what you do - makes them feel connected to you. It helps them get to know you, learn to like you, and trust that you are who you say you are and know what you're talking about.

And you know that people only buy things from people they know, like and trust, right?

To help get your storytelling juices going, here's my story:

My name is Alicia Forest and perhaps the best way for me to explain what I do is to share a defining moment in my life.

In 2001, I left a job where I was very successful yet very miserable, my marriage was falling apart, my dad was diagnosed with cancer, and my brother was getting married to a woman I had never met - in Finland.

On that trip to Finland, standing with my father on a street corner in the middle of nowhere, the weight of it all crashed in, and I lost it. Now, I am the daughter of a long line of longshoreman, and losing it is not part of our make-up. My father put his arm around me, pulling me close, but he didn't know what to say. That was the moment that led me to where I am today. When I lost everything I had invested my heart and soul into, and the strongest man I knew didn't know how to help me, I understood in that moment how very responsible I was for my life, as it was then and how it would be in the future.

So, I got divorced, I started my own business, and I am pleased to say that my dad's still with us today. Oh, and that woman my brother married became a wonderful sister-in-law and friend.

I've also found and married the love of my life, we have two amazing kids, and I continue to run a very successful and fulfilling coaching and training business that I love.

As a result of these experiences, I decided that I would dedicate the rest of my professional life to helping others create their own successful and sustainable priority-based business, in less than part-time hours, by sharing all that I've learned and by being a champion for their dream.

****

Your answer to that question is your Center of Authenticity, and offering whatever it is that comes up for you in that answer is one of the easiest roads to building your own successful and sustainable 6-figure business. (This will also help you as you define your niche a little later in this book.)

So, what's your story? Use mine as a template and start writing yours now. You may be surprised by what you learn, not only about yourself, but also about what potential business(es) may evolve for you from your story.

Guess what? That's it – Step 1 is complete! If it seemed too simple, you are either on the right road already or you need to do some more inner digging. Only you'll know which.

But if you're ready, let's move on to Step 2...

STEP 2

The Power of a Niche: Who Are You Most Meant To Serve?

Your mission is where the world's deepest hunger
and your heart's greatest gladness intersect.
~ Richard Bolles

Now that you have an idea of what your unique message is, let's move onto the second part of the Online Business Breakthrough Formula: Your Niche. Let's figure out who (your niche) is most meant to hear it (your message).

The Online Business Breakthrough Formula:

Your Unique Message + **Your Niche** + Your Niche's Problem + Your Solution Packaged = Your Profitable Product/Program/Service

Let's get something out of the way first:

You may be afraid to choose a niche for your product or service. I know there can be the fear that you're limiting your business if you narrow your niche down too much, but that simply isn't true. Believe me, it's so much easier and profitable to market to a smaller portion of the market (just think how many people there are in the world!) than to try to be all things to all people. And you'll be amazed to find out that you actually open yourself up to possibilities that would not have come up had you not focused on a specific section of the marketplace.

5

Lots of solo services professionals struggle with this issue. All you want to do is give your gifts to the world, and making decisions that make you feel as though you are saying 'no' to a segment of the population may not feel right to you. But by choosing to focus on a certain segment of the population, you are ensuring that your work actually gets out there, and you will be astounded at what comes your way as a result.

For example, even though my niche is solo service professionals, once I started defining my offerings for and to life and business coaches, my business took off. Currently, I have about 80% coaches and 20% other solo service professionals as clients. Once I started focusing my marketing efforts on my niche, all these other potential clients (who are not specifically coaches/consultants) showed up. I promise this will happen for you. You just need to keep putting your work out there, just in a more focused and consistent way via a focused and consistent message.

If you keep in mind the infinite abundance of the Universe, understanding that you can't (nor should you) serve everyone is a bit easier to embrace.

Think about the billions of people in the world. Even if you wanted to, you couldn't possibly serve all of them – and you certainly couldn't please even the smallest percentage. Trying to do so really dilutes your genius work, your best work, instead of allowing it to truly help those people you are meant to serve – your niche.

Here's why else it's best to choose a niche:

1. Your marketing gets a whole lot easier.
2. It's much easier for people (your clients) to talk about you because they understand that you do one basic thing for one group of people.
3. It's much easier for clients and colleagues to refer you for the same reason as #2.
4. It's much easier to build strategic alliances, joint ventures and partnerships.

5. It's much easier to become and be considered an expert at what you do.
6. Other opportunities WILL present themselves.

When you focus your efforts and energy on one niche you are directing the Universe to help draw those ideal clients to you. When you continue to put yourself out there with one clear message, those ideal clients will hear it and seek you out. Exciting, isn't it?

Just one more thing – even if you already have a niche, don't skip this step. It's very likely this will help you define it even further, which will ultimately create a more profitable business for you much more quickly.

NOTE: This is a lengthy chapter because most service professionals seem to get stuck here, so I wanted to make sure I gave you several of the best ways for defining your niche.

Before we go any further, let's look at what mistakes to avoid when selecting your niche. One is not being specific enough. The narrower your focus, the easier your marketing will be, and the easier it will be to attract those ideal clients to you. It may take you a few months to a year or more to narrow your niche, so don't wait to move ahead until your niche is more defined. Just be aware of the 'who' and 'what' that you work with that bring you the most enjoyment and excitement as your business grows.

On that same theme, try not to be too broad. If you try to be all things to all people, you won't be able to serve any of them particularly well.

I also want to caution you to be careful of trends. If you're thinking of creating a new service based on something that's 'hot' right now, make sure you do your research to make an educated guess that it's something that will be sustainable over the long term, so you're not picking a trend that's on its way out.

And finally, nothing is a stronger repellant of potential clients than the desperation of needing them. This might take a bit of faith if you're just starting out in your service business, but I can personally attest to the fact that letting go of my desperate desire to fill my coaching and consulting business has created a demand for my one-on-one services that I cannot meet, which means I have a waiting list of clients who want individual coaching with me. That's a nice problem to have, right?

Something else to think about as you are defining your niche is to remember that your niche has to be deep enough to support your business, meaning there needs to be a viable market for your product or service. So, yes, you want to narrow your niche as much as you can, but you will also need to make sure that there are enough clients or customers to support and sustain your business now and into the future. (We'll cover how to do this a little later in this book.)

The following are 8 proven strategies you can use to select and narrow a niche, so the odds are in your favor that if you don't know who you're best suited to serve right now, you will by the end of this chapter.

1. Quick and Dirty Way to a Niche
2. Quick and Dirty Way to a Niche II
3. Do Some Inner Investigation
4. Use Your Past Experience as a Springboard
5. Develop Your Passion into Your Unique Business
6. Follow Your Dreams, Then Show Others How to Do the Same
7. Identify Your Ideal Client
8. Still Stuck?

Bonus: The Most Effective Way to Choose a Niche

Tip: A question I'm often asked is if it's ok to have more than one niche. Yes, but you need to be very clear about each of them so potential clients are not confused. And my coach's request of you is to stay open and aware of who shows up for you as clients who you enjoy working with the most as a clue to committing to a niche.

Once you know who or what your niche is, and you can articulate it to others, you will become memorable to them, instead of being lumped in with everyone else who provides a similar service that you do. You'll begin to attract your ideal clients, the ones who will rave about what it is that you provide. And that is your ultimate goal.

Warm-Up Exercise: Put Your Thinking Cap On…

Answer the following questions in your notebook. Don't worry about coming up with the perfect answers; just jot down anything that comes to mind and see where that leads you.

- What is it that you want to become known for?
- How do you become one **in** a million, instead of one **of** a million?
- What makes you distinctive from the rest?
- What makes you stand out from the crowd?
- Why do people choose you?
- Who are you best suited to serve and why?

Taking some time to consider and answer these questions will help you get started in discovering who you are most meant to serve – who your niche is.

Tip: Ask your current clients these questions to help you in discerning the answers.

Now that you're in the niche-discovery frame of mind, let's dig deeper…

What is a Niche? And how do I start finding mine?

There's no shortage of information out there about how to define your niche. But let's keep it simple to start. The following is the basic definition of what you need to know to define your niche.

A niche is a group of people who

1. **have common issues and problems, and who**
2. **hang out together in some organized fashion.**

Makes sense, right? Now, if you want to use a few more criteria that will help you narrow down the best niche to focus your efforts on, a more profitable niche will also have:

3. **A Membership List.** Meaning, there is an association or organization attached to it, with preferably a large number of members (but not too large – see #4).

For example:
The American Screenwriters Association
http://www.asascreenwriters.com/
Professional Photographers of America http://www.ppa.com/

4. **Profitable niches are big, but not TOO big.**

For example, 'women business owners' is too big of a niche. They have many different challenges and needs to be met, in many different segments of that market. If you can't identify a specific problem(s) to be solved, it will make your work that much more difficult. It will make marketing a lot harder, and it will be challenging at best to attract those ideal clients to you.

Tip: When building your service business online, having a clearly defined niche is particularly important because the words you use to describe who it is that you work with, your chosen niche, become your 'keywords.'

You'll use your keywords in your website to optimize it for the search engines, if you run a pay-per-click campaign, and when you submit articles for publication (see Step 5 – Generate Traffic & Build Your List), as well as in many other marketing tasks. Keywords are how people find you online, so they are very important.

The 8 Strategies to Defining Your Niche

Strategy 1: Quick & Dirty Way to a Niche

a.   Give yourself some labels.

Think of all the roles you play in your life and write them down.

For example, here are some of my labels (in no particular order):

Woman	Irish-American
Business owner	Former teacher
Married	Certified SCUBA diver
Mother of 2	Aries
Singer	Swimmer
Sailor	Runner
Marketing Expert	Redhead

So, what are your labels? Make a list in your notebook.

b.   Review your answer to the Center of Authenticity question.

'What has happened in your life, good or bad, that would be most useful to share with others?'

This is a great question for you to start defining a potential niche. Review the answer you wrote down in your notebook.

c.   Do Keyword Research

Use a free keyword search tool like Keyword Spy to find out how many people are looking for your keywords each day.

Your results will show how many searches were made on that particular keyword or keyword phrase during a specified time period.

Start your research by entering a keyword or keyword phrase that describes the niche you're interested in serving. Use the work you've done so far as a jumping off point.

Keep doing this for several of your keywords and keyword phrases and jot down how many searches were done on each of them in your notebook.

When you're narrowing your niche to a certain segment of the population, you want to see about 10,000 searches on your keyword to decide whether it has the potential to be a great niche for you (ex. photographers, doctors, teachers).

Then when you're narrowing your niche down to providing a solution to a segment of the population, you want to see at least 1,000 searches on a keyword or keyword phrase (ex. time management for work-at-home moms, pet care for busy professionals, administrative assistance for chiropractors, editing for aspiring authors).

You can reach 10,000 or 1,000 by adding up the searches on the related keywords/keyword phrases that the keyword research tool gives you.

Combining these two search results will lead you to the most effective way to choosing a profitable niche. It's a horizontal and vertical approach, where your niche is where these two data points intersect. The 'who' is the horizontal and the 'what' is the vertical.

Now that you've completed Strategy 1, you should have a great direction to start moving in.

Let's take a look at Kerri as an example:

Kerri is an aspiring photographer. Her dream is to make enough money to live the life she's become accustomed to that's been supported by her 9-5 job as a production manager from her photography instead.

She understands that she needs to choose a niche in order to increase her chances of success and make her marketing that much easier. So she does the research described previously.

She uses a keyword research tools like Keyword Spy and types in 'photographers' to find there's at least 30,000 searches, so she knows her services are in demand, but how does she stand out? By scrolling through her search results, she notices that there are 3000+ searches for children's party photographers, so she makes a note of that. Here is a potentially lucrative niche for her.

She takes that information one step further and does some more online research to discover challenges that people have when finding and/or hiring a professional photographer for their children's parties. From that, she learns that many parents are most concerned about finding someone who is exceptionally good with small children, in getting them both to relax and smile and look like they are having the time of their lives, as well as being able to take beautiful photographs.

With six siblings and 22 nieces and nephews and grand-nieces and nephews, Kerri knows she's very good at working with children, and better yet, she enjoys it. She already has a portfolio of photos from years of taking photographs of her extended family at parties and other events.

At this point, Kerri could follow this lead into a profitable niche for her photography business and likely do quite well. Ultimately, she'd like to travel the world taking scenic photographs, and creating a business around children's party photography could be just the ticket that gets her there.

Now you should at least have a general idea of the direction you're heading in for a very good niche for your business. If it's still feeling fuzzy for you at this point, move on to Strategy 2.

Strategy 2: Quick & Dirty Way to a Niche II

1.   Choose a profession.

Pick a profession: massage therapists, dentists, maid service, plumbers.

2.   Research where they gather.

Visit online discussion and social networking groups at:

Yahoo: http://groups.yahoo.com
Google: http://groups.google.com
Facebook: www.facebook.com
LinkedIn: www.linkedin.com
Ecademy: http://www.ecademy.com/

Company of Friends: http://www.fastcompany.com/cof/index.jsp (associated with Fast Company magazine)

TIP: For more, visit: http://www.onlinebusinessnetworks.com/directory.html

Then search the categories of groups to find people in the profession you've chosen. Just enter the name of the profession in the search box and see what comes up.

Then use the same technique to find organizations and associations of your potential niche via Google. Go to www.google.com and search on 'profession name + association' (for example, 'healing arts association'). This is where you can find if your chosen profession has the membership list we mentioned earlier in this chapter.

You can also find a group related to your profession and/or the professional associations that would be interested in your offerings at:

http://www.ipl.org/div/aon/
http://www.marketingsource.com/associations/

So you don't have to try to remember what you discover with your research, organize the information by jotting notes in your notebook.

Continue this research for as many potential niches as you want. Some groups of people will feel more 'right' to you than others, so put a star next to those ones. Also, when you find a group that seems like a really good fit or that you want to investigate further, save the web page URL in your favorites folder in your browser and jot down the URL in your notebook.

A general rule of thumb with regard to this method of choosing your niche: You want to be able to identify at least 10,000 people within a group, organization or association that you can join, in order to have enough depth and breadth to build a business around it. You can reach that number by adding up the number of members of more than one group, organization or association as well.

3.   Participate in discussions on their discussion lists or forums

Join the groups that most interest you, begin reading the discussions, and start posting questions as well as answers to the questions posted by others. Get involved in the conversation.

At this point, you've accomplished three things:

1.   You've become more knowledgeable about this niche.
2.   You've discovered how to find and reach out to them.
3.   You have enough information to decide if it's a viable niche to build a business around.

With this work, you've basically chosen a niche, at least to start with. Then to get a better idea of who your ideal client is within that niche – remember, the more specialized your niche, the more potential profit for your business - continue on to Strategy 3.

Strategy 3: Do Some Inner Investigation

You probably have already gone through exercises similar to this one. But I encourage you to give this one a whirl. Try to respond from your gut, and not your mind, and see what comes up for you.

Have you ever wondered what your purpose is? Of course you have. We all have – at least those of us who haven't known it since birth. We all want to believe we're here for a reason, that we do have a purpose to serve.

There was likely a point in your life where you knew (or thought you knew) what your mission in Life was, but it seems like Life may have thrown you off-course.

But somewhere in you is the knowledge of why you're here... and your 'why' is as unique as you are. Remember your unique message work we did in Step 1? Let's go a little deeper with that now.

You see, there are people, many people, who need you, who need to hear your message, because they can only hear it from you, in the way that only you, as a unique human being, can put it out there.

So, right now, think about your previous clients. (If you don't have any previous clients, then think about the people in your life whom you've helped.)

In your notebook, describe each of them in detail. Put a star next to any commonalities among them. From what profession did your most enjoyable clients come from? What type of client seems to come to your door? What challenges do they share?

Next, write down your work history. What industry or business were you in? Who were your customers? Take a look at your resume and see if anything jumps out at you.

Sometimes just doing simple exercises such as this can cause an 'aha' moment, where the group you're supposed to serve becomes very clear.

It could be that your niche is actually bigger than what you've been considering. Or it may be that it's a bit smaller, too.

Add any thoughts that come up for you in your notebook. Then move on to Strategy 4.

Strategy 4: Use Your Past Experience as a Springboard

Let's take a deeper look at some of your initial thoughts from Strategy 3.

Many people start a business related to their past job experience and skills. If you've enjoyed the work you currently do or have done in the past, then it's entirely possible to create your own business from that experience.

And if you don't quite know what you want to do (your service business) or with whom you want to do business (your niche), one way to discover both is to take a look into your past to see what things and people have interested you over the course of your life. This will help you to access potential areas where you could offer your work.

Many of us had dreams when we were children about who and what we wanted to be. Sometimes those dreams weren't encouraged, and other times they fell by the wayside due to circumstances beyond our control.

Let's revisit those dreams now:

In your notebook, complete the following exercises:

Step 1a. Carve your life into 5 year increments and answer the following questions for each:

- What did you love to do? (draw, color, pretend to be a teacher)
- What were your favorite toys, activities, hobbies, interests, etc.? (coloring books, skating, being on or near the water)
- Who did you do those favorite things with? (self, lots of friends, Dad)
- Who did you admire? (Mom, a certain movie star)
- What did you want to be when you grew up (at each age, if it changed)?

Step 1b. Think about the jobs you've had at each stage of your life and answer these questions:

- What did you love about the work itself?
- What did you not love about the work itself?
- What was it about the structure of where you worked that you enjoyed? (time off, flexible work hours, supportive colleagues)
- What was it about the structure of where you worked that you did not enjoy? (scheduled hours, limited time off, unsupportive environment)

TIP: Answering these questions will also help you define how you want your own business to operate.

Step 2. From the work you did above, make a list of 20 things you like to do, that are appealing, challenging and interesting to you, whether or not you are doing them currently.

Step 3. Now write 10 things that were positive about your work experiences, and that you would like to incorporate into your own business.

Step 4: Read through what you've written and notice what and who stands out for you. Your 'what' has the potential to be the area in which you give your gifts to the world. Your 'who' has the potential to be your niche. Jot those down in your notebook as you review what you've written.

Rediscovering a dream or a passion, or simply realizing what work is meaningful and important to you will move you forward in your path to defining the kind of business you want to have as well as the type of people you want to serve. It's an inspiring process that should ignite some excitement for you!

Strategy 5: Develop Your Passion into Your Unique Business

In Strategy 4, you identified a number of areas that are both meaningful and important to you. Wouldn't it be fantastic to develop a business from your passion?

What is it that you would love to give to the world? Is it your skills of a certain service? Is it your knowledge having gone through something unpleasant and come out on the other side stronger and wiser for it? Is it a product or service that you know would help other people live a better life, make more money, or ease their stress?

Are you passionate about horses and want to open your own boarding and training facility? Or are you passionate about having a clean house and want to write and publish a book full of tips to help others keep their homes neat as a pin? Have you been a volunteer? What parts of your volunteer work did you truly enjoy? Was it public relations, event planning, financial management? What about those can you envision as a business?

In your notebook, work on the following exercises.

Step 1. Think about those passions, hobbies or interests you wrote about in Strategy 4.

Step 2. Choose one or two that most resonate with you. Write those down in your notebook.

Step 3. Pull each of them apart until you get down to the smallest version of what they can be. Jot down those down in your notebook.

For example, let's say your passion is cooking and your ultimate dream is to write and publish a cookbook, but the task seems too daunting at the moment and you know little about publishing. You could start small by offering cooking classes in your home. This will build your confidence and your credibility, as well as give you real world experience about what works and doesn't work for the average cook, which will be invaluable for that cookbook you want to write. Having a successful track record as a cooking instructor will also help you immensely when you pitch your book to a publishing house, if you decided to go the traditional publishing route.

You can easily build a business online from this example, by offering a content-rich newsletter, hosting a membership site, or offering lessons via video, for example.

Step 4: What is one small step you can take in the direction of your dream? Write it down in your notebook.

As you travel on this journey, each small step will allow you to further define what it is that you want and don't want. And your niche, your area of expertise and the audience with whom you wish to share that expertise, will unfold.

I promise that if you take that first step, the inspiration and momentum will build. Each small step will lead to the next, and with patience and persistence, your niche will become evident.

Strategy 6: Follow Your Dreams, Then Show Others How to Do the Same

Don't you love stories about people who have followed their dreams and turned them into reality? I particularly love to hear stories about people who have developed a dream into a successful business. Not only are they are wonderfully inspiring, but they prove that it's entirely possible too.

My dream was to build a successful business from home before my husband and I started our family, and I have done just that. I didn't do it overnight, by any means, and I learned a lot along the way. And now, I've built a very successful business from following my dreams and showing others how to do the same.

Are you on your way to turning your dream into a reality? What are you doing now that you can take the experiences and knowledge you've gained and turn into a profit-center for you?

For example, one of my colleagues coaches dentists on how to operate a more successful dental practice. From his experience in doing so over the course of several years, he decided to use what he learned from building his own successful coaching practice ($1 million annual gross) and develop a second niche of coaching coaches on how they can build a successful coaching practice of their own.

Your niche would include others just like you (which makes them very easy for you to describe and find). For example, maybe you're a freelance writer and you're writing articles on a fairly consistent basis for a handful of publishers in a certain industry. You may not be where you eventually want to get to (being assigned articles as opposed to writing query letters, for example) but you do have the knowledge and experience that got you to the point of success you are currently enjoying. Why not package that wisdom into a product or service to offer to others? You could host a website with tools and resources for that niche and charge a membership fee. Or you could write and sell an e-book about the things you wished you had known (even 10-page e-books can be profitable). Or you could write and self-publish a step-by-step book based on your experiences and offer that to your niche.

In your notebook, develop a niche from something you already know by following these steps:

Step 1. Think about what you wrote down for Strategy 5 about the work you do or have done, the knowledge you've gained, and the experiences you've had.

Step 2. Choose one or two things that you feel you could share with others, having 'been there, done that.' Write them in your notebook.

Step 3. Brainstorm how you can develop those things into a niche business. See the examples above for inspiration. Jot down your ideas in your notebook.

Step 4: Choose one or two of those ideas and start exploring your options for developing them.

As I've said before, the narrower your niche, the easier it will be to market your products and services. If you start out with something small, like an e-book or a 30-minute audio about '10 Things You Need to Know About… (fill in your expertise),' you'll be able to market this to a niche that is clearly defined for you already. Who are the people in that niche? They are You… when you were where they are now. So share what you know. I promise there are people out there just waiting for your words of wisdom.

Strategy 7: Identify Your Ideal Client/Customer

Another way to help define your niche is to identify your Ideal Client/Customer. If you've ever had a client/customer who was more trouble than they were worth, then you know how important it is to create boundaries around whom you will and will not do business with.

Maybe you've had a client/customer who was constantly on the phone to you, never satisfied with your product or service, but just kept coming back to complain. Maybe you've had a client/customer who didn't pay on time – ever. Maybe you've had a client/customer who demanded far more than you were offering. You might even remember an inkling from the first time this person came into your business that something wasn't quite right.

One way to avoid situations like these is to create your Ideal Client/Customer Profile, and refer to it every time someone wants to do business with you.

Use your notebook to create an Ideal Client/Customer Wish List.

As you do this exercise, visualize your Ideal Client/Customer. Who is it that you want to do business with? Be specific about the kind of people you want to serve.

Step 1. Start with the basics. What are the basic characteristics of your Ideal Client/Customer? For example, what are their demographics - gender, age, salary, education, location, etc. Write those down in your notebook.

Step 2. Who are your current clients/customers? For example, are they artists, work-at-home moms, small businesses, dentists, restaurants, etc. Write it down in your notebook.

Step 3. What are the values of your clients/customers? If you currently have clients/customers, think about the things that you enjoy the most about them. For example, are they fun to do business with, do they seem to like what they do, are they honest and reliable, etc. Write those values down in your notebook.

Step 4. What do your clients/customers do? For example, are they working on getting to the next place in their career, are they trying to build a business of their own and need and want to sell products, do they serve the same niche you do, etc. Write it down in your notebook.

Step 5. How do your clients/customers respond to you? For example, are they respectful and considerate in communication with you, do they rave about your services, do you feel appreciated by them, do they regard you as an expert, etc. Write it down in your notebook.

Step 6. How do your clients/customers treat you? For example, do they pay on time, are they on time for meetings, do they have reasonable expectations of you, etc. Write it down in your notebook.

Step 7. What is it like working with your clients/customers? For example, do you look forward to interacting with them, do you want to help them succeed, are you stimulated by the work you do together, etc. in your notebook.

Step 8: Take what you've written and craft a paragraph or two that describes your Ideal Client/Customer in your notebook. This is your Ideal Client/Customer Profile.

Here's some of what makes up my Ideal Client Profile:

- Are positive, optimistic, fun to engage with
- Don't complain, blame others, or have a victim complex
- Are doers, take action, move forward quickly
- Have a big vision, and are confident they can make that vision a reality
- Have reasonable expectations of themselves as well as of me
- Are respectful, asks for clarification, communicates easily
- Shows up ready and open for our work together
- Is able to easily afford my fees and pays on time

Bonus Step: Review your current client list against your Ideal Client Profile. You may find that perhaps you need to let a few clients/customers go. This will create the space for more of those clients/customers who are ideal for you. For any new clients/customers, make sure you use your profile as your guide before you decide to do business with them.

Once you're clear about who your ideal clients are (and who they are not), you're putting that intention out to the Universe to help attract those people to you. As a group, they are your Ideal Niche. By developing this profile, your niche becomes much easier to describe to others. Marketing, reaching out to those whom you want to serve, becomes exciting and intriguing as you seek out your Ideal Client/Customer, instead of a frustrating and overwhelming process.

Tip: This step is very useful if you are already clear on the 'who' of your niche to help you weed out those clients who are less than ideal for you and your business. Take time to do this exercise now to boost your bottom line sooner.

Strategy 8: Still Stuck?

As I said at the beginning of this step, lots of new business owners get stuck here more than anywhere else when starting out.

If you've reached this point and you still feel stuck on your niche, let's try something different.

Although in this book, defining your niche comes before discovering what it is that they want and are willing to pay for (what problems they are having that they want help solving), sometimes it helps to let things happen backwards.

For example, if you work with clients from diverse groups, is there a common issue that most of them seem to grapple with?

Does time management seem to be a common theme, or work-life balance, or lack of understanding of technology, etc.? What problem do you seem to be helping to solve most often?

This can help to lead to defining a niche for your business.

Write down the common challenge in your notebook, then begin to be aware of the 'who' who most struggles with this. For example, perhaps you're a virtual assistant who works with small businesses. You have clients in several industries, but there seems to be some common challenges that they all struggle with, things like delegation, managing email lists effectively, and addressing customer service issues in a timely manner. You could retool your marketing messages to address any one of these challenges specifically, which will lead those small businesses with that specific problem to you. You become known as the expert, managing your own business becomes much easier because your service is more focused so you are more easily able to streamline your processes and therefore be more effective, and you'll make more money.

You now have 8 proven and strategic ways for discovering and defining your niche for your ideal business. Do the work, see what comes up for you, follow your instincts, your heart, your gut, and your desires, because that is what will build a successful and sustainable 6-figure business for you.

I want to encourage you to really work the strategies until you gain clarity around your niche. But don't wait for it to be perfect or exact; just trust your feelings around it.

For some people, a niche leaps into their lap. But for most of us, it takes some time to hone it. Start serving whatever market feels the most right to you right now, and then continue to pay attention to the clients and challenges that most excite and energize you. And give yourself some time - your niche will become more clear over time as you and your business evolve.

****

In the first section of this chapter, you've worked on discovering and defining your niche. Now you're ready for the next step in the Online Business Breakthrough Formula – to find out what your niche wants so you can create it and offer it to them.

The Online Business Breakthrough Formula:

Your Unique Message + Your Niche + **Your Niche's Problem** + Your Solutions Packaged = Your Profitable Product/Program/Service

Now that you've figured out your niche (or you've at least narrowed it down significantly), let's figure out what problems they are struggling with, and what they want by way of solutions.

To get you started with creating a new income stream that you can pretty much guarantee will actually bring you money, you need to find out what it is that your niche wants so you can create it and offer it to them.

If you do that, they are much more likely to buy it, aren't they?

It's important to note that if you create products/programs/services that YOU think your prospects need - offerings that seem the most logical to you that will help your prospects do, be or have better - you might find it very difficult to sell any.

There are two things you need to remember when creating any offering for your niche:

1.   **People buy what they want, not necessarily what they need.**
2.   **People buy based on emotion, not necessarily on logic.**

I'm sure you can think of examples from your own life where these two statements were true.

So if you're trying to sell them what you think they NEED, you might not get a very good response because your offering might not be necessarily what they WANT.

So, in order to serve your niche well, meaning in order to give them what they want, you need to know them well. Even if you are one of your niche (if you're like me – a coach who coaches coaches as part of my niche), you need to keep on top of what's going on in your niche, what's being talked about, what challenges they are facing, and what their current needs AND desires are – because that information will pave the way for you to create offerings for them that they will buy.

Tip: If you are at a point where you are clear about your niche market and you're focused on it, you will want to continuously ask your niche for what it wants so you can continuously supply it. If you will only ask your niche, it wants to help you create the services, programs and products it wants to buy!

Let's dig a bit deeper into this, as it's critical for you to understand and implement this thinking in order to create a successful and sustainable business much more quickly and easily.

There are three important factors to creating a profitable offering for your niche:

1. Always know your niche before you begin to sell them anything.

Get inside their heads, feel what they are feeling, enter the conversation in your niche's mind, and intimately understand the problems that your niche is experiencing. The more you are able to do that, the more effectively you'll be able to create what it is that they want.

2. It's not what you want to sell that matters. It's what your niche wants to buy that matters.

It's actually irrelevant what it is that YOU want to sell to them – at least in the beginning of your relationship with your potential client or customer.

You may have already learned this lesson. I know I have, where I got so excited about creating something that I thought would be great for my niche, and I went ahead and put it together, and then watched in dismay as hardly anyone bought it.

On the flipside, when I created the 21 Easy & Essential Steps to Online Success System™, I was asking my niche all along what its biggest challenges were, and asking them what they wanted, and then I continually asked them what they wanted so I could be certain I provided it for them - and my results that time were hugely different. During the initial launch, over 40% of my email list bought the 21 Steps System (which is a very high conversion rate by Internet marketing standards, by the way!) and it's still my bestselling product today.

3.   **Give them what they want now so you can give them what YOU want later.**

The deeper or more advanced work your client may need will come later – I promise.

Tip: Never put together a complex product like a multi-media package or live event before making sure it's something that a significant number of your niche, particularly those on your own email list, have directly expressed interest in enough to invest in.

How exactly do you find out what your niche wants? Do your research.

There are several ways to get this information and use it to help you create an offering that will solve your niche's problems and make a profit for you at the same time.

One of the great things about working on the Internet is that we can do some market research relatively quickly and for free (or very inexpensively) to get the information we need to see if our idea for a product or program is one that the people in our niche are interested in buying.

Tip: Make sure you conduct market research of your niche on an ongoing basis. You want this to be an ongoing part of your marketing plan so you can keep up with the changing desires of your niche and continue to offer them what they want (not what you think they need).

If you keep surveying your niche, it will take you much less time to create something and bring it to your market than if you have to put your project on hold while you find out if it's a worthwhile endeavor.

So, ask them, listen to their answers, and THEN create your product.

Let's get into the nuts-and-bolts of how to do this. I'm going to give you 7 proven and highly effective techniques to do this, so you'll have some to choose from that you feel will work best for your particular niche.

1.   Simple: Ask them!

Ask your prospects a simple, open-ended question, like 'What's your biggest challenge with building your business online?' or 'What's the one thing you'd like to learn more about that relates to balancing your work and family life?'

Tailor the question to your niche and use the information you receive to help spark ideas for your new products and services.

For example, I do this when people sign up for my free gift and ezine at http://aliciaforest.com. I ask them what their biggest challenge is about building their business online via an autoresponder (an email that's automatically sent from my email list service when someone signs up for my mailing list). From the answers I received, I created the 21 Easy & Essential Steps to Online Success System™, my List-Building Secrets product, as well as many of my other offerings. And I've got a list of other potential products that have been sparked by those answers as well.

What happens is that over time you'll start to see the same responses over and over, the same struggles, challenges, questions and problems will keep coming up, and the solutions to those are the ones that have the highest potential of being a profitable product for you.

To help you create your question to ask your niche, here are two different types that have been tested as the most effective, with examples of each.

I learned from Tony Robbins years ago that people tend to orient their lives around things they either want to move toward or things they want to move away from. Using this psychology in your question can elicit the most fertile response from your niche.

Here are the two types of questions to use that will help you discern your niche's most pressing problems, using this thinking:

Type 1: This is the moving away from question.

'What is the single biggest challenge you are experiencing when it comes to X?'

You can ask for as few or as many problems as you want, but you'll get more responses if you ask your niche what their single biggest challenge is. And obviously, replace X with your niche.

For example:

What is the single biggest challenge you're having as a wellness coach?

What is the biggest problem you're experiencing when it comes to closing a sale?

What is the one thing you're having the most trouble with as an adult with ADD?

Type 2: This is the moving towards question.

'What is the one thing you would like most when it comes to X?'

Again, replace X with your niche.

For example:

What is the one burning question you would like answered when it comes to your real estate career?

What is the one thing you would like most like to know when it comes to homeschooling your children?

What's the one thing that would help you most when it comes to writing your first book?

Once you have your question, you need a vehicle with which to ask it. You can put your question to your niche as an autoresponder when they sign up for your Free Taste (we'll talk about this later in this chapter and in Step 4); periodically in your ezine; ask them on your teleclass and have them email you their response; or ask them on discussion boards, forums and lists, and blogs in your niche. You can ask them by phone, face-to-face, or via social media.

If you're looking for more places to ask, go to Facebook, LinkedIn or Google Groups and type in keywords for your niche to get a sense for what groups are out there where you can join in on their conversation and ask the members your question. Group members are usually very willing to share with you their biggest challenges and desires.

2. Do a simple survey that asks 2-10 questions using a survey tool like Survey Monkey.

This allows you to ask more specific questions to elicit more specific responses. Doing a survey like this really helps you to not waste your time creating offerings your niche simply doesn't want. Post your survey via the same vehicles as listed in #1.

Tip: This can also be done as a second step to the asking them the one-question strategy. Take your responses and put them into a survey as potential products, ask for their level of interest, format preference, and then ask at what price point they'd be willing to pay. The responses you receive will help you offer just what your market is willing to pay for.

3. Set up a separate website where you direct traffic to ask your question.

Create a one-page website and put your question and a space for an answer in a simple form. Your web designer can create the page with a form, or most web hosts have the scripts available for simple forms like this available for free for their customers' use.

Compose your question like this:

Dear X,
What's your biggest question about X?

Thanks,
Your name and URL

For example,

Dear Entrepreneur,

What's your biggest question about using search engines to market your business?

Dear Work-At-Home Mom,
What's your greatest challenge with running your business from home?

To increase the number of responses, consider offering a free gift in exchange for their feedback. You have to make sure the script you're using captures their email address or you ask for it. You could also offer another valuable gift, like a short ebook or audio download. Keep it simple, though. Something like a checklist is usually good.

You can direct people to this website via your email signature and by promoting it in your ezine as well. Another very effective way to get a larger response is to use Facebook Ads or Google Adwords, social media, and search engine optimization techniques to direct a lot of traffic to answer your question.

4.   Do an Ask Database campaign

The Ask Database service allows you to set up your question however you want (via your ezine, a separate website, as an email signature, etc.). Then with the code it gives you upon signing up, Ask will collect your feedback, store it in a database, and then you can search within that data.

For example, you can search for the keywords or keyword phrases that occur the most to extract the information that is the most useful to your product creation.

Tip: Ask is like having a dedicated search engine for the results that you're collecting, which is really powerful because your responses give you written copy that you can then turn around and use on your sales pages, which can cut your sales page writing time in half.

I'll share a secret with you – by using the responses you're getting from your question in your sales pages, you're also doing something that is going to make a dramatic difference in the number of your sales – which is that you'll be answering your potential buyer's objections in your sales letter, which makes it almost impossible for them not to buy from you, because you're speaking their language.

Ask Database is a web-based service, so just go to www.askdatabase.com to sign up for a free trial, get the snippet of code that you need to put on your website, which is the code that generates your question and gives you the form that your visitor fills in with their answer. Then that data goes into your account's database at Ask Database, which you can access anytime. You can export your data, so you always have access to it, even if you've decided that you've gotten enough information over a certain period of time and want to cancel your subscription.

Here's an example of how powerful this can be. If you use the 'word density' tool, you can search for the one word that appears the most in your response. Then that's the one word that becomes part of your headline, or is part of the title of your ebook or audio.

This is one of my Sales Copy Secrets:

All of these approaches are in essence getting your market to tell you exactly what it is that they want. If you listen properly and use the language your niche is using, you can feed that right back to them in the form of sales copy and products.

To further the point, when you create your product, you'll want to use the questions and the responses that people gave to tell you exactly what to answer in your product. When you tell your potential buyer what they will get, what's in it for them (WIIFM), you make the buying decision much, much easier for them.

Whatever words or phrases that come up the most are the ones you'll want to put as your top bullet points in your sales letter. When you actually sit down to write your sales letter, you can go back to your survey results and use the real words that people used when they answered your question.

By using the same phrases as they do, you'll make writing your sales copy so much easier. And you'll be speaking their language, making it all that much simpler for you to relate to them and make the selling process much less work.

You can invite people to the link for your question through the same avenues I've mentioned previously - via email, forums, discussion lists, other people's lists, your website, your blog, your email signature, and Facebook Ads or Google Adwords.

Tip: If you're focusing on a niche, you should always be polling because you'll find trends and hot topics that you can respond to very quickly.

Tip: You could do a second step as research and to increase the ultimate success of your offering as well: Send a draft of your results (your product you've created in response to your survey question(s)) to the people who responded and ask for their feedback.

You could simply say, 'Here's my draft – what other questions would you ask? What would you do to improve it?'

Then ask, 'If you found the information helpful, would be you willing to provide a testimonial?'

Tip: When you're asking what it is that your niche wants, don't underestimate the important of the emotional charge that's behind their struggles. If you listen to what your niche shares with you about the emotions they have around their struggles, you can use that information to create a deeper connection to them in the content of the product itself. Remember that people don't necessarily buy based on logic, but on emotions instead.

You can address those emotions in the sales letter. Doing so can make a big difference in the ultimate success of your product. The response from you, by way of how you address both the emotional and practical sides of solving their problem, shows that you've really listened to your niche.

5. Ask for feedback on all programs and products you offer.

One of the best (and sometimes most courageous) things you can do to continue to improve your offerings is to ask for feedback from your clients and customers. You can set this up as an autoresponder to go out after a certain period of time has passed after someone's bought your product or participated in your program.

Your best bet is to ask for some general feedback as well as some specific comments to inform the next iteration of that product or program to continually make it better suited for your audience.

6. Create an R&D team of people in your niche.

A classic example of finding out your niche's problems first-hand is to create an R&D team comprised of people in your niche.

Ask your email list for volunteers to join your R&D team, then send them this one question to start:

'What do you wish you had known before you became a/an X?'

Because you've asked people to have a special relationship with you by inviting them to be part of your R&D team, you'll likely get much higher quality feedback and more responsiveness from them.

After you've asked them your introductory question, you can start to utilize them more by further asking them for specific comments on their compiled feedback. From this information you can create a list of potential products to provide the solution to their responses to your question.

Be respectful of your R&D team's time and limit your asking to a handful of times a year. Also acknowledge their help and show your appreciation by offering something of value to them as a thank you.

7.   Read, read, read…

Subscribe to industry periodicals, websites, other ezines in your niche, business magazines (Entrepreneur, Fast Company), review other experts' surveys of your niche when you come across them, and books specific to your niche. Keep your finger on the pulse of what's happening in your niche by continuously reading.

Now you have 7 ways to discover what it is that your niche wants. Asking your niche what it wants is the beginning of building a relationship with them. It's also the absolute foundation that will create wealth for you.

By the way, implementing this process is a great way to self-moderate and focus only on those things that will bring you an abundance of clients and cash. If you find you're very creative and have lots of ideas, you can test first to see if it makes sense to continue putting time and effort into any one idea, which really helps to set your priorities.

Remember, your niche will tell you what it wants, if you'll just ask them!

Now let's take what you've learned and move on to…

Creating What Your Niche Wants

I know you're probably anxious to get started on creating your for-fee (read: paid) product or service offering, and we'll cover that in Step 6. Right now, though, I want you to start thinking about what you want to offer as your Free Taste, your first free offering, which is a taste of what it is that you do, to entice people to sign up for your email list.

This is a critical step for building your business online. You want to give your prospects a taste of what it is that you offer in exchange for their email address, so you can start to build a relationship with them. Without that relationship, you don't have a business.

I recommend that your Free Taste be a mini ecourse, special report or a mini ebook or checklist, or a short video or audio. We'll talk about offering your ezine (online newsletter) – which is critical to your relationship building – a little later, but I suggest you develop something simple for your first Free Taste.

Creating and offering a Free Taste of what it is that you do is the first step in creating your Online Business Breakthrough Marketing & Product Funnel.

Once you have an idea for your first Free Taste, use your notebook to sketch an outline for it. As you continue to work your way through this book, keep adding your thoughts, ideas, and content to your outline. That way, by the time we get to the actual production of your Free Taste in detail, you'll be ready to hit the ground running.

Just a quick reminder here:

The Online Business Breakthrough Formula:

Your Unique Message + Your Niche + Your Niche's Problem + **Your Solution Packaged** = Your Profitable Product/Program/Service

Once you've figure out what your niche's problems are, you can create or find (by doing the necessary research) the solutions to solve those problems. That's what your work up until now has done. You now know what's keeping your niche up at night, and you can use that information to create the solution for them, both free and paid.

For example, my best-selling product, 21 Easy & Essential Steps to Online Success System™, is a perfect example of this process. I asked my niche about the things they struggle with in building their business online. One of their biggest challenges was basically how to get their business online, from scratch, without a lot of technical know-how, and on a budget. As I put 21 Steps together (the same system I follow and that you basically hold in your hands with this book), I kept asking questions to make sure that I covered everything they wanted to know. I started out with general questions, and then dug deeper until I really hit the nerve about what was bugging them.

Tip: I want to make an important point here: The responses I got to my questions were the responses from MY list, comprised of people who have opted to be part of the Online Business Breakthrough community. So even if you are offering very similar services that I do, your results from YOUR list might be very different, because they are made up of different human beings.

I actually love that about this process – it means that you and I can tailor our offers very specifically to our very own audience. Doesn't that make everything just so much easier?

Earlier in this chapter, your goal was to find out what concrete problems your niche is struggling with by asking them. Your goal now is to develop and offer concrete solutions to those problems.

Once you've pulled your solution together, you can package it in a variety of ways: as an ecourse, a PDF manual, an ebook, an audio or video download and/or CD, DVD, etc.

Tip: Not to belabor the point, but it bears repeating, and I'd hate for you to get frustrated by creating what you think your niche needs, instead of what it wants (and therefore will buy). You want to make sure that, as you're putting your solution together, you're collecting the information that solves the problems your niche has told you it wants solved.

We often think we know what our niche wants. And sometimes we do. But don't let yourself make the mistake of packaging what you think is important into a product (ex., an ebook) without making sure that you are creating what your niche wants.

If you meet your clients where they're at, you'll have a much easier time building a successful and sustainable 6-figure business. Once they start buying and using your products and services that solve the problem they want solved, they will be much more willing to continue down your Funnel towards higher ticket items that you really want to offer them.

This may be a shift for you, but I strongly encourage you to embrace it. It will make everything about building your business, and your customer's loyalty, that much easier.

Again, as you're compiling your solution, you'll want to decide how you'll package it. There are so many ways to do this that I couldn't possibly cover them all within the pages of this book, but I will cover the most popular ones in Step 6. For now, here's a short list of how you can package your offerings:

Ebooks	Audio Downloads/CDs
Ecourses	CDs/Audio Tapes
Ezine	Memberships
Print books	Joint Ventures/Strategic Alliances
TeleSeminars/Webinars	Affiliate Programs
Live Workshops and Seminars	Livestream/Ustream
Speaking Gigs	Video
Group coaching	TV

Then how you've decided to package your product will determine how you'll actually deliver it to your niche. Some delivery systems only do one thing, but most overlap, so it makes sense to think about your bigger vision for your business as it grows and make the investment in some of the systems that do several things if you can. More about this a little later.

Tip: After you finish reading this book, take the time to start investigating which service providers you are going to use, using aliciarecommends. com to help you.

For example, if you are going to offer an ecourse, then you'll need an autoresponder service to deliver it to your subscribers. For this, you'll want to look into an email list service like Aweber. Yes, there are other good autoresponder services out there, but I've personally used and think Aweber is the best and has very competitive prices. They offer a 30-day free trial, so you can sign up and start playing around to see if you like it.

Or if you are going to record an audio download, you'll want to sign up for AudioAcrobat's free 30-day trial so you can start playing. And yes, there are other audio service providers out there, but I personally use AudioAcrobat and think it's one of the best recording services available, and their prices are very competitive and reasonable.

Start compiling your solution and keep filling in your Free Taste outline in your notebook. Then decide on the packaging of your Free Taste – are you going to offer an ecourse, an audio product, an ebook? Finally, research service providers for your packaging as necessary, sign up and start playing.

Here are some examples for you to model:

1. If your niche is helping first time authors to publish their book, your Free Taste may be a 10-page ebook titled 'The Ten Mistakes to Avoid When Writing Your First Book Proposal.'

2. One of my past clients who offers financial planning services offers a recording of an audio interview she did about tax planning as one of her Free Tastes.

3. Another client who is a virtual assistant offers a free report where she shares her 10 favorite marketing resources as her Free Taste.

   Tip: My clients are doing this all the time. For more ideas, examples and help – join us with your special invitation found at the end of the book.

4. I offer a special report and audio interview that walks the reader through these 6 steps in very simple terms.

Now that your creative juices are flowing, let's move on to…

STEP 3

Create Your Compelling
Marketing Message

Using the work you did in Step 1 to discover your unique message and Step 2 to define who you were meant to share that message with (your niche), it's time to create your compelling marketing message for your business so you can start gathering that niche to you.

Answering 'So, what do you do?' Effectively

Remember in Step 1 when you answered the Center of Authenticity question? Let's use your answer to that question to help you articulate what you do to others.

Being a service professional, sometimes it's difficult to come up with an answer to the 'So, what do you do?' question that is both exciting and interesting. In order to entice people to want to know more about your work, whether they are a potential client or not (but they probably know someone who could be), you want to leave them with a memorable experience. You want to be able to answer this question with a simple but compelling statement so they will ask the next question, 'Really? Tell me more…'

Promise me right now that you'll stop answering this question with, 'I'm a _____.' Why? Because when people are looking to hire someone, they really don't care what you call yourself - they just want to know that you can solve their problem.

For example, if you're a massage therapist, saying, 'I'm a massage therapist' is not particularly compelling. The person asking you already has their own idea of what a massage therapist is and does. However, saying, 'I help stressed-out men and women remember what it feels like to be relaxed and refreshed, instead of frazzled and wiped out all the time,' will likely prompt them to ask, 'Really? Tell me more...'

Ask your current clients what benefits they receive from working with you. You may be surprised by their answers, and those answers will help you craft a compelling answer to the 'What do you do?' question. When you ask your clients this question, ask them to think past the superficial. Ask them to get to the root of what value your service gives to their lives. Ask them to describe the benefits and results that they get from working with you.

If you're new in business and you don't have current clients to ask this question to, ask your colleagues or your coach to help you flesh it out.

In your notebook, write down the benefits and value your clients receive from you. If you don't have clients yet, what benefits and value are you committed to your future clients receiving from you?

Once you've gathered what value your clients receive from you, you can create your 30-second introduction. Your 30-second intro is your compelling and concise answer to the 'So, what do you do?' question.

I work on a 'conversational' version with my private clients, but this one comes in handy for email signatures and in certain brief exchanges, and it's actually easier to start out with as well.

Here's an easy template for you to follow:

'I   (work   with/teach/educate/inspire/support/consult/coach/etc.) _____ (your niche) who struggle with _____ (your niche's problem) _____ and who would like to _____ (your solution).

Here's are a couple of examples:

'I teach solo professionals who struggle with not having enough clients the 6 simple steps to attracting an abundance of clients, consistently and easily.'

'I teach solo service professionals the 6 simple steps to marketing their business to 6 figures in half the time they could on their own.'

'I mentor women entrepreneurs to break through to 6 figures and beyond so they can live the life they ache for.'

'I mentor women entrepreneurs to build a priority-based, highly profitable business in less than part-time hours.'

That usually leads to the 'Really? Tell me more!' which is when I launch into the rest of my 'pitch', something like…

'I teach through private and group coaching, online and over the phone, as well as via several written products, like my 21 Easy & Essential Steps to Online Success System. Here's my card with the website address where you can find out more and get a copy of my free special report that walks you through my process.'

In your notebook, start working on your 30-second intro.

Then, when someone next asks you what you do, give your 30-second intro instead of saying, 'I'm a _____.' Make a mental note of what kind of reactions and connections you make. Then tweak as necessary until you devise an answer that feels and sounds really 'right' to you. You'll know when you've hit it.

Please don't skip the exercises in this step because it lays the foundation for the steps that follow.

Now that you've got your 30-second intro either nailed down or very much in the works, let's apply it in a practical sense to your business identity or brand.

Think about your business for a minute. What is it about it that makes it different from the rest of your competitors? Not just what makes it as unique as you are, but what makes it different? And I mean different in the sense that you are catering to a specific market or niche.

Just as you devised your 30-second intro to use for networking purposes, we're going to do the same thing for your business brand. Consider your previous work on what makes you one 'in' a million, instead of one 'of' a million. For example, if you are a virtual assistant and someone Googled 'virtual assistant' in their search to hire someone, what is it that makes you stand out from all the other VAs out there?

I'll tell you: It's EVERYTHING that makes your business uniquely yours... and that includes everything from your website (does it immediately draw visitors in?), to your business name (does it tell your visitors what you offer?), to your tagline (which helps to clarify your offer), to your business card, to your in-person appearance, to your voice mail message, to the tone and style of your emails and email signature.

So what common message or theme do you want to put out there? What is it about all of these things that you can tie in together? Because you must put out a consistent message so you don't confuse your audience.

Make sure your theme (for example, 'more profit in less time', 'live your best life', 'stop your divorce now') is abundant in every marketing message you put out.

Doing so lends credibility, and it helps to establish you as an expert in your field, because you know what it is that you are offering and that makes it that much easier for potential clients to want to work with you.

People prefer to work with specialists, with those who have expertise in the area in which they are struggling. If your message is clear, then they know what you stand for, they know why you're different, and they end up feeling much more confident and comfortable that you know what you're doing.

People hate to make mistakes and feel stupid. Your goal is to reassure them that they made the right decision in working with you or investing in your offers.

So make sure you have a common theme throughout your marketing messages, something that makes your business uniquely you, something that sounds and feels like YOU.

An effective way to convey your area of expertise and who you are best suited to serve is by either having a business name that says it, and/or by including a business tagline that spells it out. This may seem obvious, but I'm often surprised by how many service professionals choose business names that leave you wondering just what it is that they do.

If you decide to name your business after yourself, then you'll want your tagline to tell your potential clients what kind of service/products you offer. So, if your business name is not self-explanatory, then you should have a tagline that is.

For example, if you're a sales consultant, and the name of your business is Jack Snow, Inc., no one is going to know what you offer. You can still keep your name as your business name, but if you do so, you want a tagline in your marketing materials that clearly tells what it is that you offer. For example, Jack Snow, Inc., Sell Snowballs in Hell Sales Training.

Here's a better one: If you name your business something like, The Coaching Business School (Chris Barrow's), then you know immediately what kind of business he's in – business coaching. And you can infer by 'school' that his program(s) encompass all aspects of running a coaching business.

But if you prefer to name your practice something like, 'Inner Compass Coaching' (which, by the way, was the name of my coaching practice when I first started out), then in order to convey what it is that you're offering, you will need to have a tagline that everyone can understand. Mine was 'finding and following your true north' – which is NOT a great example of this! You could guess that I was life coaching, but, unless you're a fan of Martha Beck, you're probably wondering what the heck is 'true north'? Again, I figured most people would have a feeling for what it meant, but it didn't really resonate with anyone but me. Lesson learned.

And without giving you the play-by-play of how I ended up business coaching, specializing in the area of marketing (although my MBA is probably a clue), the name of my first coaching business was Client Abundance, which is pretty clear, but just in case, my tagline was 'More Clients, More Money, More Freedom'. Anyone visiting my website or reading my business card would know that I teach people how to get more clients for their business, make more money and create more freedom.

And know that what you decide today doesn't have to be IT forever. My current business is now my name (aliciaforest.com) because I've grown enough of a reputation and platform to build upon it. My tagline evolved as well, to 'Mentoring women entrepreneurs to build a priority-based, highly profitable business in less than part-time hours'. Your tagline will likely go through some iterations before you settle on one that really resonates with you and your niche.

When choosing your business name, think about how to clearly get across what it is that you offer, within the name itself or at the very least, in the tagline.

Your business name and tagline is part of your compelling marketing message. It's your BRAND. And it will go on every piece of marketing you send out.

So decide on a business name and tagline, and start using both on all of your marketing materials and in all your business interactions.

Now that you've got your business name and tagline down, let's move on to…

How to Choose and Register Your Domain Name(s)

You can't have a website without a name for it (called a domain name) and it's not something you want to have to change later, although you can, if you must.

Tip: I always recommend registering your own name in addition to your business name, if it's different, as well. You never know how famous you're going to get, and you don't want to have to pay someone else for your own name as a domain name, right?

Registering domain names is easy and cheap. I register my domains with my webhost (Dreamhost) and enom.com.

What's important to remember when choosing where to register your domains is that you want to be the owner of those domains. Web hosts don't always work out and if you want to move your site to another host, you need to be able to take your domain name with you. So be sure that you maintain ownership of your domains, no matter who you register them with.

There are a couple of things to think about when deciding on your domain name:

1. If you make it 'keyword-friendly,' the search engines will rank you higher. This isn't something that will make or break your business, as it's not as critical as it once was, but it's something to consider.
2. For example, if your domain is <u>www.livewithpurpose.com</u> then your relevancy factor goes up because people who are looking to live their lives with more purpose will likely put those words in the search box. But if your domain is <u>www.bluespirit.com</u> there's no relevance because no one is going to search for 'blue spirit' when they are looking for information about living their life with purpose.
3. If your business name can be easily misspelled, you might want to consider another name. But if you don't want to use another name, it's best to register any common misspellings as domains, too. You can have them point (redirected) to the correct domain down the road. For example, my client Kim's business name is Mystique Event Planning – www. MystiqueEventPlanning.com. Some people, when typing in her business name (assuming they heard it somewhere) may easily miss the second 'e' between 'mystique' and 'event' so she also registered www.mystiqueventplanning.<u>com</u> so she doesn't lose a single prospective client.

Go to your notebook and make a list of the domain(s) you want to register. Then go online to check their availability and to register them.

Tip: I'm often asked if it's necessary to register .net or .org or any of the other extensions, but my experience has been that it's not necessary. But if it makes you feel better and because it is so inexpensive to register a domain, feel free to register your domains with as many of the extensions as you want.

Just a quick review. So far you've:

1. Figured out the unique message you were meant to share in the service of others.
2. Defined your niche and discovered the problems your niche wants solved (and started thinking about and outlining your first FREE product – your Free Taste), and created a compelling marketing message/brand.
3. Decided on a business name and tagline and registered your domain name(s).

Now you want to start filling in your Online Business Breakthrough Marketing & Product Funnel.

STEP 4

The Power of a Free Taste, an Invite Site, and a Constant Connection

Your Free Taste – Part I

First you'll need to attract prospects into the top of your Funnel. You'll do that by creating your Free Taste - an ezine, mini ecourse, ebook, report, guide, or checklist, etc. - and by putting a sign-up form 'above the fold' and prominently on your Invite Site, which we'll cover in this step a bit later.

Once you have prospects in your Funnel, you'll want to find ways to give them more valuable content at increasingly higher prices as they go through the Funnel.

For example, the second level of your funnel might offer an ebook for $27 or an ecourse for $39. The third level might have a home study course for $147 or a series of teleseminars for $77 each. The fourth level might offer a boot camp for $247, and the fifth level might offer your one-on-one services for $500.

We'll fill in the first level of your Funnel when we cover creating and delivering your first for-fee product, but first we want to start building your email list of potential clients and customers by attracting them into your Funnel via your Free Taste. We covered this a bit earlier in this book, but let's get into the details of exactly what a Free Taste is and how powerful it can be in building your successful and sustainable 6-figure business.

Offering your prospects a taste of what it is that you provide is a proven and easy way to get people to become part of your community, and part of your Funnel. By offering them a sample, you're giving them an opportunity to get to know you with very little risk.

In your Funnel, the taste you are giving your potential clients is at the top of the funnel, the widest part. The taste is your freebie/complimentary/gift offering and is your first (and usually only) opportunity to engage your prospect. Your taste needs to be something of value that you offer for free to people who visit your website in exchange for their contact information, usually their name and email address.

This is often one of the most overlooked steps in building an online business. A prospect needs to see your message many times before they will feel confident enough to risk handing over their money to you. And in order to build a relationship with people you need to be able to contact them again, which means your goal is to capture their email address before they click away from your website.

If they leave, it's unlikely that they will come back, so don't lose the opportunity to welcome them into your community, into your Funnel. They landed at your website because they were looking for something (usually a solution to a problem they are having, right?). Give them a taste of the solution you offer. And remember to make it easy for them: make your sign-up form so obvious that they'd have to trip over it not to notice it (yes, that includes pop-ups and the like, because even if they annoy you as much as they do me, they work).

So, what can you offer of value in exchange for their email address? An online newsletter (ezine), an ecourse, an audio clip, or a special report, are all good options. Personally, I like the offer of an ecourse, audio, special report or ebook AND an ezine (make sure you've told them that when they sign up for your Free Taste, they will also get your ezine). That way you give them a taste of what your services are like with the ecourse, audio, video, special report or ebook, and then you keep in touch with them on a regular basis with the ezine. The ezine allows you to build a bond with your readers in a uniquely personal way, letting them get to know, like and trust you over time, without you having to build that bond one-on-one.

I want to caution you not to offer any one-on-one interaction with you at this level. You want to leverage your time, and offering free consultations or one-time meetings with you is not a good use of your time. Let them get to know you through your Free Taste. When and if they become serious about you and your products or services, they will move further down the Funnel (from free to fee, from potential client to paying client) without you having to 'sell' them on what you provide during a complimentary session (how nice is that?).

So what is your Free Taste going to be? Here are some other ideas:

1. Write a Top Ten article about the benefits of your products and services, convert it to a PDF file, and offer it as a special report.
2. Record a short audio about the three key things your niche needs to know about X.
3. Create a mini ecourse that encompasses the five steps to getting started for your market.
4. Or create a quick-start guide that helps your market focus on how to get started.

Once you've given them a taste, they will likely come back for more, eventually turning from a prospect into a client.

Let's use the work you started in Step 2 to complete your Free Taste.

Take out your outline from your notebook and decide what your Free Taste is going to be. Remember, it should a solution to a problem your niche wants solved.

Tip: If you've been thinking about or working on a big idea, choose a chunk of it to use, or create a summary overview of it, using the ideas listed above.

Delivery System for Your Free Taste

How you've decided to package your Free Taste will determine your delivery system. As I mentioned earlier, some systems do only one thing, but most overlap, so it makes sense to think about your bigger vision for your business as it grows and make the investment in some of the systems that do several things if you can. But also know that it's not necessary if you're just starting out and funds are tight – it won't hinder you a bit.

Tip: Just a reminder note, though: Whatever you do, DON'T deliver your offerings manually. Just don't do it – you won't be able to keep up, it is a waste of your time (which equals money), and it will only frustrate you further when you try to make a switch to an automated delivery system later.

Below are the ways you can deliver each of the most common types of a Free Taste:

E-courses via autoresponder:

Aweber: http://snipurl.com/aweberautoresponders
1ShoppingCart: http://snipurl.com/shoppingcart1

Ecourses are basically emails that are set up and sent automatically via autoresponders. To get the emailed ecourse, you have to subscribe to it, usually by filling in a form with your name and email address which subscribes you to the autoresponder, or by sending a blank email to an autoresponder email address.

For example, when someone visits my site at http://aliciaforest.com there are two boxes for my visitors to enter their information if they want to receive my free audio interview, '6 Simple Steps to a 6-Figure Solo-Business, even if you're starting from scratch'. One asks for their name and the other their email address. Once someone enters their info and clicks on the 'Get my free audio now!' button, they are automatically subscribed to my list. They then start receiving a series of emails that I've written previously and set up to go out at various intervals after the initial confirmation email.

Once you have an account with an autoresponder service, it's easy to set up your first autoresponder.

PDFs:

If you are going to offer a special report, guide, checklist, ebook, or other PDF file, you want to use your word processing program (like Microsoft Word) to create it, and then convert it to PDF.

Ezine:

For your ezine, my suggested services are Aweber, 1ShoppingCart, or InfusionSoft.

TIP: Again, I don't recommend that your Free Taste be an ezine, but that you offer an ezine in addition to your Free Taste.

Audio:

If you are going to offer an audio recording, then get AudioAcrobat: http://snipurl.com/foraudioacrobat

This service will walk you through step-by-step on how to record and publish the recording online. Recording with Audio Acrobat is a breeze, and it may be particularly favorable to those who'd rather talk than write, and who don't want to figure how to record over the computer (although with Audio Acrobat, they show you exactly how – you can't mess it up). But another option they give you is recording over the phone. You get your own recording phone number and PIN to call to record whatever you want. With a click of a few buttons at Audio Acrobat, you'll be recording like a pro.

Video:

If you're going to offer video, even your smartphone camera will do to get you started. You'll need to host your videos online, and most people start out with posting to YouTube, because it's free and because it's the second most used search engine, which can increase the number of people who will view it. You can also host videos with Audio Acrobat, Vimeo or Viddler. (See aliciarecommends.com for more.)

Tip: You might want to consider adding written content to your audio and/or video Free Taste as well to remove any technical barriers that an audio/video offering might come up against for your listener.

Now you've got your Free Taste completed, or nearly so, it's time to create the place where your prospects can find and sign up to receive it, welcoming them into your Funnel. That's where your Invite Site comes in...

Create Your Invite Site for Your Free Taste

Ok, it's time to build your first Invite Site, where you offer your Free Taste in exchange for your visitor's name and email address. Your Invite Site is a simple 1-page website.

At this point, you've registered your domain name. Now you need to choose the web host who will host your website (if you didn't register via your chosen host already). I'm going to make this process super-simple for you. There are many good hosts out there, but for what you need now and to take you well into the growth of your 6-figure business, there's only one I recommend.

I recommend Dreamhost (see aliciarecommends.com for link) – another service I've been using since 2001 and have been very happy with. There are many good hosts out there, so if you decide not to go with Dreamhost, know that you still don't need a host who charges more than $10 per month, ok?

Tip: Dreamhost's basic plan – Crazy Domain Insane – is all you need to start with, and will likely be all you'll ever need.

Even if you choose Wordpress, you still need to host your site in a webhost's servers. Once you've chosen and purchased your web hosting plan, you can create your Invite Site.

Your Invite Site is just that: a one-page website that contains some copy to entice people to sign up for your Free Taste (again, so they enter your Funnel and get on your list). You can see the one that took my business to 6-figures the first time at www.ClientAbundance.com.

Why is it important to capture your visitors by getting them on your list? Because these are the people who are your potential clients and customers, who are telling you that they are interested in what you have to offer. These are your 'warm' prospects in sales-speak, the people who have raised their hands to tell you they want more from you. These are the people with whom you'll build a relationship over time, and to whom you'll market your products, programs and services. These are the people who will become your paying clients and customers.

The idea with the Invite Site is to start building your list now, and to start building your relationship with your subscribers now, so when you have for-fee products, programs and/or services to offer, you have a ready audience to offer them to.

You may have heard the saying, 'A confused mind says no.' Meaning, don't give your visitor more than one decision to make when they visit your site. There should be no question about what you want them to do. And that is for them to enter your Funnel by signing up for your email list via your Free Taste.

Haven't you visited a site and been so overstimulated with so many options that you didn't stay long enough to figure it out? Don't do that to your visitor. When you're at the beginning of building your business online and your email list of potential clients and customers, only give them one choice - signing up for your Free Taste.

The first thing you'll need to decide is if you're going to create your site yourself or if you're going to hire someone to do it for you, regardless of whether you decide to use a blog platform like Wordpress or go the traditional HTML route.

Tip: Regardless of whether or not you are going to put together your Invite Site yourself, one of the best investment you can make in your online business is learning how to make quick and simple changes to your site yourself (and with Wordpress, it's really easy).

You'll have to decide which web authoring software you will use. For my HTML sites, I use Dreamweaver, which has a steep learning curve, so unless you're already familiar with it, or have a capacity for such things, I don't usually recommend this program to start with. If you're creating an HTML site, I recommend Macromedia's Contribute. I haven't used this software myself, but my non-tech-savvy clients tell me it's fairly easy.

However, if you've decided on using the blog platform like Wordpress for your Invite Site, then you might want to play around with it a bit before hiring someone to design it for you.

Eventually, you may want to hire someone to create your logo (if you don't have one already) to add to the header (top) of your Invite Site; in the meantime, you can create a perfectly acceptable header using one of the free or paid Wordpress templates.

If you decide to hire a web designer, (even if you barter services for it), make sure you outline what you're looking for in your Invite Site. This should help you keep costs way down. Really, for your Invite Site, you could hire a college or high school kid to do it for you for very little money.

What do you need on your Invite Site?

1. Enticing copy about your Free Taste.
2. A sign-up form for your Free Taste (code provided by your email list service)
3. Your contact info
4. Photo of you and/or your Free Taste. These are optional but can help to make you and your product feel more 'real' to your visitor.
5. Title, Description, and Metatags with your keywords/keyword phrases (a web designer with a marketing mindset will know what these mean and how to implement them).

The one thing you MUST have is a way to capture the visitors to your Invite Site – see #2 above. Regardless of how you've decided to package your Free Taste, how you'll capture your visitor's name and email address is the same via a simple script you copy and paste provided by your email list service.

For example, if your Free Taste is an ecourse with a subscription to your ezine and you're using Aweber as your list service, the script you need to put into your website (the code that goes into the HTML source box of either your HTML web page or your blog page) will be provided by Aweber. But don't worry, it's really simple to cut and paste the code into your Invite Site.

Tip: These are the kinds of things you'll want to learn how to do - cut and paste short pieces of code to make your website really work well for your business, even if that means hiring a high school or college kid for an hour to show you how.

Tip: Adding a testimonial or two to your Invite Site will help to encourage people to sign up for your list as well. Ask a few of your current clients for a results-based (what their challenge was before working with you, what specific progress they've made since working with you) testimonial and their permission to post it on your site.

STEP 5

Generate Traffic & Build Your List

Once you have completed your Free Taste and set it up to go out automatically via the sign-up form on your Invite Site, your next (and always) priority is to start generating traffic and building your list. Everything you do going forward should include a tactic for getting people on your list. Since this is vital to your success, I'm giving you **57 proven and effective ways** to do this.

**Always remember: Your list is your pot of gold.
Treat them very well!**

Strategy 1: The Location of your Sign-Up Form

The very first list-building strategy you should implement is to take a look at where your sign-up form is located on your website. Is it buried, hard to read, or does your visitor have to scroll to find it?

You want to make sure that when someone visits your site, they know exactly what to do first – and that's to get on your list. Make it super simple by following these steps:

1. Make sure the location of your sign-up form on your homepage or Invite Site is 'above the fold,' meaning your visitor does NOT have to scroll down to find it.
2. Make sure that it stands alone, meaning minimize any additional text or graphics around it.

3. Place your sign-up form front and center on your Invite Site page, or in the upper right-hand corner, if you are adding it to an existing site.

Studies have shown the same results, and to be honest, I think they are about neck-in-neck in effectiveness as well, so choose what looks and feels best for your site.

Reminder: Make sure your Free Taste is a compelling enough offer so your visitors sign up. Usually a free ezine alone is not enough (but that's not always true), so consider offering some instant gratification by way of a mini-ecourse, special report or checklist to encourage people to sign up.

Strategy 2: Make signing up super simple

For your opt-in box:

1. Ask for your visitor's First Name
    This allows you to personalize your messages, which increase open rates (meaning that more people will actually read your message).

2. Ask for Primary Email
    This also increases open rates, and ensures that your message actually gets through to your subscriber.

3. Have a sign-up button that says 'subscribe' or 'send me the _____ now' This makes it obvious what your subscriber needs to do to get on your list.

4. Include copy that tells them they will receive a copy of your ezine or some other regular publication.
    You want to be sure to tell your subscriber that they will be hearing from you on a regular basis, so you are managing expectations from the beginning of the relationship.

5. Include a simple privacy policy, like 'We will never share your email address, period.'
   This assures your subscriber that you are not going to spam them.

RECAP: The point is to not ask for too much information when asking people to initially sign up for your list. If you need more, you can get it later.

Have your sign-up form be short and sweet. Just ask for your visitor's first name (so you can personalize email to them) and their primary email address (which can cut down on the number of undeliverable email addresses you get).

It's been widely tested that asking for those two pieces of information will get you the most response.

Strategy 3: Use Pop-Ups

Make it easy for your website visitors to sign up for your Free Taste by offering your sign-up form as a pop-up, which you can do very easily with Aweber or a stand-alone pop-up software like PopUp Domination.

As much as we may find them to be an annoyance, testing shows that using a pop-up can increase your opt-ins by as much as 70%.

There are different types of pop-ups: when someone first visits your site, when they leave, ones that swoop in from the side after a few seconds, ones that pop- up at the bottom, etc.

My preference is the exit pop-up, which pops up after you leave a website, and that is set up so it knows whether I've seen it before or not.

Strategy 4: Collect 3 Testimonials for your Free Taste

Few things are more powerful than testimonials from people who have benefited from your offerings. And they are something you should always pepper throughout your website and your sales copy.

If you can add one or two testimonials to your Invite Site, you'll increase the sign-ups to your lists. To collect testimonials:

1. Ask those people who have sent you unsolicited positive feedback about your Free Taste if you can have their permission to quote them in your marketing materials. Offer to add their name and whatever web URL or other brief contact info they'd like to supply, and remind them that it is added exposure for them as well to be displayed as a testimonial to your offering.

Here's a sample script for you to model:

Hi (name),

I wanted to send you a quick note and tell you how much I appreciate the kind and wonderful words you emailed me about X.

I wondered if you would be willing to allow me to use your comments as a testimonial on my website?

If you'd be agreeable to this, just hit reply and send me an email with your name, company name and website URL that you'd like posted with your comments.

Oh, and if you have a photograph you would like to include of you, please let me know.

If you have any questions, don't hesitate to ask.

Thanks so much!
<followed by sig>

2. Ask directly for testimonials from your ezine readers and clients who have purchased your products or service.

For example,

Dear (name), I hope you've enjoyed the ecourse, '(name of ecourse here).'

I want you to know that your feedback is very important to me, and I'd greatly appreciate it if you could take a moment to send in your comments/suggestions for improving the mini-ecourse.

Also, please let me know if you'd be willing to have your comments posted as a testimonial on our website to encourage others to sign up. Since I'm passionate about reaching as many people who are as passionate about working successfully for themselves as I am, your words may be just what they need to give Client Abundance a try.

If you are willing, that's fantastic! Simply reply to this e-mail and indicate your name, e-mail address and website URL you wish to have posted with your comments.

Thanks so much!
<followed by sig file>

These are just examples to get you started – use your own words and voice for best results.

Strategy 5: Offer a bonus for signing up

This is in addition to your Free Taste.

Sometimes people need more enticement to give up their email address. To improve your chance of getting people to sign up for your list, offer then something of added value as a bonus. It can be something of yours or something by someone else that's of high quality and use to your target market.

Whatever the bonus is, it should be a 'set it and forget it' offering. In other words, it should not require more time than the one block you use to create it, if it's something of yours, or more time than the one-time setup required of offering something by someone else.

You might also want to consider giving away something that upsells to one of your other offerings. For example, give a discount coupon towards one of your products, programs or services (but not your 1:1 work!).

Strategy 6: Email Sig

If you're not using your email signature at the end of EVERY email you send, you are missing out on using one of the best no-cost 'pull' marketing devices you have at your disposal.

Your 'sig' can easily be created in most email programs, or your can use a free contact service like Plaxo to create an HTML version. Just know that a text sig is just as good and easier to create and change than a HTML version.

For list-building purposes, your sig can direct people to your Invite Site, your dedicated page to sign-up for your Free Taste and ezine or other periodic publication.

You probably send dozens of emails a day. If you add your sig to each email you send, you'll be able to put your marketing message out subtly just as many times.

Another bonus to using an email sig in every email you send is that email often gets forwarded. You never know where it may end up or who is on the receiving end who may also sign up for your list.

What should you include in your email sig? 3 things:

1. your name and title
2. your business name and tagline

3. DEFINITELY INCLUDE your promo for your Free Taste by including a brief enticer with a link to more information (always include the 'http://' even though it seems cumbersome, as some email programs will not redirect you without it. Again, make it as easy as possible for someone to click successfully through to wherever you want them to go).

Here's one of my sig lines:

Alicia Forest, MBA
The Business Shifter™
Ready for your Online Business Breakthrough?
www.AliciaForest.com

Another version to use if you are sending out an email to your current subscribers or those in your target market already is to put your sig in a PS format, as in:

cheers,
Alicia

PS: If you're interested in building a 6-figure business based on your passion for serving others and haven't signed up for *Shift* with Alicia Forest (my ezine that's packed with useful tools and tips to attract all the clients and customers you want and so much more), you may want to do so now. Just visit http://www.AliciaForest.com. As a bonus, you'll also receive my FREE audio interview, '6 Simple Steps to a 6-Figure Solo Business, even if you're starting from scratch!'

Strategy 7: Quick Question

Using the Quick Question market research technique can also be used to build your list. Ask the people in your target market a simple, open-ended question, like 'What's your biggest challenge with building your business online?' or 'What's the one thing you'd like to learn more about that relates to balancing your work and family life?'

Ask on forums/discussion groups/blogs in your target market with a link to your Invite Site.

This strategy works very nicely because the people who are interested in responding are likely to also sign up for your list. Make sure you offer them a link to do so with your question.

Strategy 8. Add your sign-up form to all your web pages

Since you never know where someone will enter your site, make sure you have your sign-up form on every page of your website. Also, include it on all your sales pages, if you have separate ones for each of your products and/or services.

Someone may not buy on the first pass (they usually don't), but they are much more likely to sign up for your Free Taste while they think about it.

Strategy 9. Optimize your website

The first step in doing any of optimization is to find the best keywords for your target market or product.

What you need to do is put yourself in the shoes of your market, and really think about what words/terms they would type into a search engine to find what you have to offer.

This can be tricky at first, so it can be helpful to brainstorm with a colleague, or better yet, gather a small group of your target market and ASK them what keywords and phrases they use to search online for what you're offering.

Get started in researching and gathering your keywords by using one of the free keyword research tools that are available to you.

Use the free keyword search tool at Keyword Spy to find out how many people are looking for your keywords each day. You want to see about 100 hits per day, or 1000 searches on your keyword/keyword phrases per month.

This will also give you a list of related keywords as well, with their search numbers, to help you build your list. You can add these up to reach 1000+ per month.

When you're building your keyword list, start with about 10-30 keywords, and think about them in terms of all of your content, not just your target market.

(This is a bit different than when you're researching a viable niche.)

Once you've got your list of keywords ready, you'll want to add them to certain places in your website, on each page, which is what will optimize it for the search engines.

1.   Title Tag:

The title page of your website should be different for each page of your website. And the title for each page should be specific to the content of that page.

Think of the title of a chapter in a book. It usually sums up what's in that chapter or gives you an idea of what that chapter is about. It's the same thing here. The title of each page of your website should reflect what's on that page, using keywords to be the most beneficial.

This is what the search engine spiders read first, so it's important to put your keywords in here. This is also the text that displays in the top blue bar of your browser window.

2. META Tags:

Definition: Meta just means 'behind the scenes' - so what's in the code on your web page that's invisible to your visitor.

Meta tags provide information to the search engines, as they "read' your web page. To draw more traffic to your site, you want to put your keywords in a meta tag.

Warning: don't repeat your keywords in your meta-tags. That's considered 'keyword stuffing' a page, and the search engines can penalize for this.

3. META Description:

Put a couple of sentences (not more the 250 characters) describing the page, using some keywords, in your meta description.

4. Content:

Incorporate your keywords into each page of your website. Because people scan when they read online, you should break up the copy on your web page, by using white space, headings, sub-headings, bullets, etc.

Some ideas of where to put your keywords:

- Page headings
- Bold and italicized text
- Bulleted and numbered lists
- Hyperlinks
- Incorporate keywords into body copy. Put your keywords a minimum of 4xs on your page. Have them near the top of the page and then sprinkled throughout in a natural manner

Strategy 10. Leverage Transactional Emails and Web Pages

As we build our online businesses, there are lots of emails and web pages that we send people to that are part of the process, like affiliate or sign-up confirmations, order information, download pages, etc.

We want to leverage these by adding an invitation, or making an offer or suggestion on each of these transactional emails or redirected web pages.

The world of list-building is characterized by the fact that you want to strike a balance between too many emails and not enough so this strategy allows us to make another offer very quietly without hitting our client or customer's inbox one more time. What we're doing is making list-building use of the emails that people expect as part of the nature of the transaction.

Basically, we want to tailor our shopping cart autoresponders and such a bit so they use a marketing or list-building mindset, instead of just a transactional, 'accounting-based' mindset.

Strategy 11. Put a 'PS' Box on your Sales Pages

A 'PS' is a short invite to join your list from your sales pages. Put a 'PS' on all your sales pages leading to your Invite Site so people can sign up for your list.

Most people who visit your sales page won't buy on the first pass, so you want to make sure you give them the chance to join your list. And you never know where someone will enter your site from - they may have skipped the sign-up page altogether - so you want to make sure they have the option to join your list.

Strategy 12. General Directories/Lists to Promote Your E-Zine

It's VERY important to have a way to keep in touch with your list, and the most effective way to do that is through an ezine.

One of the best and proven most effective places to list your ezine for greater distribution is at:

The Directory of Ezines.
http://snipurl.com/doezines

There are two ways to use this service:

1. List your ezine

Although DOE is accepting new submissions at this writing, you must have a minimum of 1000 subscribers, and you must be willing to do one of the following:

a. accepts ads
b. accepts articles
c. accept joint ventures

If you're not at 1000 subscribers yet, you can still use this service to...

2. Search for other ezines:

-   for potential ad swaps
-   joint ventures
-   article submissions
-   ad placement
-   and other ezine publishers can do the same for you once your ezine is listed

E-Zine and Website Announcement Lists

I also recommend that you list your ezine at:
New List at http://new-list.com

This is a one-time submission only, and it's a free service (run by Chris Knight of EzineArticles.com) that helps you get the word out about your ezine in a targeted way.

New-List allows you to get a free announcement of your ezine to a targeted list of folks who have asked to receive prompt notifications of when New-Lists (new ezines) are created. This is not 'spam' (which is the sending of unsolicited emails), but rather the sending of new-list announcements to opt-in lists that folks have asked to be on. All together, 16,000+ members receive New-List announcements via email.

The benefits to announcing your list with New-List is that it's great and fast exposure for your list, it's free, thousands of folks who are interested about your topic will hear about your new list, and many list directories owners are on many of the New-List lists, which means your New-List submission may also get listed in their lists of lists, giving you additional free exposure.

Strategy 13: Interview with Experts

Conducting interviews of people in your target market whose name is familiar to those people in your target market is one of the most effective list-building strategy for building your list FAST.

Here are two ways to do this:

1. You can interview them over the phone or video and record it, offering the audio/video as a way to entice people to sign up for your list; use it as your free taste or extra bonus (and you can ask if your interviewee would be willing to do the same - most will).
2. You could do a written interview via email and offer the written transcript as a Free Taste or bonus to those who sign up for your Free Taste.

Here are 3 steps to making this strategy work for you in your list-building efforts:

(1)   Make a list of about 15-20 well-known people in your target market who you could potentially interview.

To find them:

1.   Top-of-mind (those you model, who are known to you already in some way)
2.   Search your inbox to see whose lists that apply to your target market that you're on
3.   Look on information websites in your target market where there are experts (like About.com)
4.   Google for others you don't know about yet
5.   Ask your networking lists for recommendations and referrals
6.   Look in your industry magazines
7.   Articles in the newspaper written by experts in your target market
8.   Who's being interviewed online – radio, podcasts, v-casts, offline TV shows

A great place to start? AMAZON

Look at books within your target market by going to Amazon.com, then search for and create a short list of authors who would be interesting to interview for your market.

(2)   Once you have your initial list, Google the name of each person.

See if they have a website and if they do, visit it and see if they have a list - you'll know if they do if they offer a Free Taste! Put a star beside the names of the people who have both a website and a Free Taste.

(3)   Compose an email (which you can use over and over) that invites each person to be interviewed by you on the topic you choose.

Obviously it needs to be a topic that your target audience is interested in learning more about. Say something like,

'I'm a follower of your work and would love to interview you about X. I'd like to share this interview with my newsletter readers, and I would provide a copy for your use as well. The interview will be conducted professionally, and I will promote it wherever and whenever seems appropriate.'

What you want to make obvious to the potential interviewee is that you are offering to give them free publicity.

Tip: Don't fret if your list is small now. If you interview well-known people in your target market who have large lists, most will happily let their lists about the interview. What's important, of course, is to have your sign-up form for your list in place before the interview is announced.

Advanced Step: If the person has a product for sale, see if they offer an affiliate program. If they do, add a second star beside their name.

The names with the stars beside them are the first people you should contact via email. Then work your way steadily down the list.

This is a very effective list-building strategy and here's why:

1.   Increased credibility.

People will talk about your interview on various lists in your target market:

'hey, there's this great interview with _____ that you can get at (your URL) that talks about exactly that...'

That generates viral word of mouth, which leads to more sign-ups for your Free Taste, for your list.

The more well-known the person is, and the better their relationship is with their list, the better for you.

2.   There is a high likelihood that the person will publicize your audio interview to their list, if they have one.

This means publicity for you and your Free Taste, again attracting more subscribers to your list. Ask them to do this – most will. Just a mention in their well-regarded and read ezine can do wonders for increasing your list numbers.

Advanced Step: If you tie your interview into an affiliate product the person has created, you can create a passive stream of income for yourself as well. So, when you ask to interview someone, tell them they are permitted to promote one of their offerings at the end of the interview.

As an affiliate of that product, you'll earn a small commission through your affiliate link that you give out on the call as well.

As you build your stash of interviews with leaders in your target market, you are becoming well-known as well. Don't be surprised if you in turn get invited to be interviewed by someone else using just this technique, which again, benefits you and your list.

And if you continuously implement this strategy (say one interview a month or a quarter), it will build momentum, and could eventually build a nice package for a future product for you to offer.

Strategy 14: Become a bonus participant

Adding valuable bonuses to your offerings is a way to encourage people to buy. As a list-building technique, you could do the same for someone else's product offering.

Make an offer of a bonus to your colleagues for their products and programs, individually and through the networking groups you belong to.

By giving a bonus for someone else's offering, you're putting yourself in front of other people's traffic. You do less work, but get more subscribers.

Strategy 15: Subscribe to 3 – 5 other ezines in your target market

This strategy will not only give you ideas for your own ezine and keep you up-to-date with what your colleagues are offering, but it will also serve as a vehicle for potential joint ventures/strategic alliances.

JV/SA's can open up whole new lists of people to you, if you are able to partner with others whose business complements yours and together create and offer something of value to both your lists.

An example of this would be an audio interview about a topic that's of interest to both your lists.

Visit www.go-ezines.com and search for ezines in your target market. Or Google 'name of your target market + ezine' or 'name of your target market newsletter' and see what comes up. You can also search the Directory of Ezines to find compatible ezines for your market.

Before you approach the author, however, you want to make sure you get to know their stuff, their style, and make sure that it's compatible with yours, as well as agreeable with your audience.

Strategy 16: Swap Ads/Recommendations with others in your target market

Seek out other ezines in your target market whose publishers might be interested in swapping ads. They can either be formals ads, or just a recommendation within the content of the ezine itself.

Again, go to www.go-ezines.com and search for ezines in your target market. Or Google 'name of your target market + ezine' or 'name of your target market newsletter' and see what comes up. Or use the Directory of Ezines for your search.

For more formal ads, instead of paying for advertising you may be able to find other publishers who would be willing to 'swap' an ad. You publish their ad in your publication and they do the same for you.

When you approach people be sure to let them know the size of your list and why you think their ad may do well with your list.

Strategy 17: Leverage Your Thank You Pages

First, a definition of Thank You Pages:

It's the page that shows up after you've subscribed to something, that confirms the subscription went through.

Here is a sample thank you page of mine – it's an old one, but it gives you a model of pertinent information you should include on your thank you page (as well as an example of how to use a 'tell-a-friend' module to increase your list numbers):
http://www.clientabundance.com/thankyou.html

Thank you pages are one of the singularly most underutilized pages on the internet.

Think for a moment: After a person has subscribed to your 'thing', they are probably the most engaged with you as they have been to date. It's a moment when if you recommend they might like to visit something else, they very likely will, which makes these pages prime real estate.

As this list-building strategy suggests, you can invite others to share thank you pages with you. Leverage the thank you page your new subscriber receives upon signing up by offering something else they might also be interested in getting.

Most people don't use their thank you pages for anything other than saying 'thanks' (and some don't even do that!). You should always offer something else (another product or service of yours is ideal) but for list-building purposes, you can utilize space on your thank you page to offer something else of value from someone else. The ideal situation is a trade, where they do the same for you on their thank you page.

You could say something like, 'Thanks so much for signing up for my ezine. I know you'll love it! And by the way, I think you'd also really enjoy X.'

Here's an example of an email doing just that. You can adapt it as you see fit.

Hi Chris,

I've been getting your ezine for awhile and think it's fabulous. I also think folks who sign up for my ezine (name here) would greatly benefit from it as well.

So I was wondering if you would like some of the thank you page traffic from my site?

I'm thinking that I can offer the link to your sign-up page on my thank you page after subscribers sign-up for my ezine at http://www.ClientAbundance.com.

If this will help bring you more subscribers, I'm happy to do it. I know my subscribers would find value in your information, and although this isn't tied to my offer, if there is a place where you think you can send a link to me from somewhere, that would be great too. I promise to treat your subscribers with respect.

Let me know what you think when you have a moment.

Thanks so much,
Alicia

Send a handful of these requests and expect that you will get some people who will say yes to your offer. Implement this strategy once a quarter and your list numbers will grow.

Strategy 18: Co-Registration

Although a bit of an advanced strategy, co-registration when done right can add loads of high-quality subscribers to your list.

From participating in a co-registration program with a handful of my colleagues, I've added over 2000 subscribers to my list.

There are legitimate co-registration services like http://www.getsubscribers.com/ or you can hire someone to set this up amongst your colleagues.

Here's an example of what one of my co-reg pages looks like: http://www.clientabundance.com/mainconfirmed.htm

Strategy 19: Be a Sponsor

Being a sponsor for an event or for a cause is a very effective way of getting in front of more of your market.

If you're planning on attending an event, see if there are opportunities to become a sponsor.

If you're a member of an organization or association, many times they will have ways in which you can promote your business via a paid sponsorship.

When being a sponsor, offer your Free Taste (plus some extra goodies if your budget allows) to entice people to sign up for your list.

Sponsorships abound both on- and off-line, so keep your eyes open for these types of opportunities to promote your business and add people to your list.

Strategy 20: Tell-A-Friend Module

Everyone prefers getting a recommendation for a product or a service from a trusted source. It means they don't have to do the research themselves, or find out whether or not something works for them through trial and error, shouldering all the risk.

The same goes for your business. And you'll get more HIGHER QUALITY clients and customers through referrals than any other method.

Three super simple ways for you to help your current clients and customers tell others about you using the Tell-A-Friend strategy.

1. Simply add a sentence or two to the bottom of each issue of your ezine or any other Free Taste you have. Something like:

    'We grow by recommendation! If you enjoyed this issue, we'd love it if you'd pass the word. Do so by forwarding this to a friend and inviting them to subscribe at the link (above/below).'

    Consider your personality and tone of your ezine or your other Free Taste for the appropriate wording for your tell-a-friend request.

    You can also offer a gift – something of value from you – to people for referring your Free Taste.

2. Put a Tell-A-Friend (TAF) feature on your sign-up thank you page.

    A formal Tell-A-Friend software can help you make it super simple for people to tell a friend about you and your product or service. Some shopping cart systems and web hosts offer this feature, so be sure to check yours and start utilizing it now to help build your list.

If your current vendors don't offer this feature (and even if they do), I highly recommend TAFPro for this. This software has a one-time only fee (it's inexpensive), plus a very reasonable installation charge if you need help from the very customer service friendly Paul Galloway, the owner.

Here's an old 'thank you' page for signing up for my ezine that uses the TAFPro software:

http://www.clientabundance.com/thankyou.html

3. Advanced Step: Having installed a Tell-A-Friend module, use it to implement a contest with prizes.
    Using the Tell-A-Friend module, you can easily take the next step and use the contest management feature in the software and create a contest page to send out to your existing subscriber list. To see an example of what I mean, visit:

http://www.clientabundance.com/contestexample.htm

Note: This is an old page I created just for an example, so please note this contest is NOT running. It's just an example for you to see what I mean.

Tailor this page to your own needs and brand but it should give you an idea of how the Tell-A-Friend module can really encourage people to point others in your direction.

Strategy 21: Give Away a Product for Referrals

In Strategy #20, we covered how to use a tell-a-friend module to increase your list numbers. To take that to an advanced level, you can offer your current list something of higher value for free for suggesting to others to join your list.

In order to make this strategy effective, offer a product that you would normally charge a fee for, and use the TAFPro software to make it really easy for your current subscribers to refer you to their networks.

My link to TAFPro is: http://www.tafpro.com/?10289

Strategy 22: Video Referral Opt-Ins

A really powerful way to build your list with video is to use it to entice others to refer their lists and networks to your video.

Here's how it works:

1. Create a mini-site with a video of you and an opt-in box.
2. In the video, talk about the next valuable and juicy video they will get once they enter their name and email address in the opt-in box.
3. Once they do that, they receive the link to the video you promised, but there's a second video they can receive if they refer 3 people to the initial opt-in page (see #1).

Tip: Don't hold back in your first video. Give them such great content that they will WANT the second video.

Strategy 23: Create Your Mini-Script

These are ways to build your list verbally in addition to writing online.

1. Use the BNI Elevator Speech template, which is more conversational in tone than most elevator speeches...

Your Mini-Script is your compelling answer to that dreaded, 'So, what do you do?' question. Your Mini-Script encourages people to ask you to tell them more about what it is that you do.

It goes like this... (tweak for your own personality and style)

You know how some (your niche or the client/customer you are aiming at)... Experience (the problem your niche is struggling with)... Which means that (the outcome of the problem)... Well I do/can do is (your job/product/service)...

Which means that (the solution)...

The benefit of which is (the outcome of the solution)... Would you like to know more?

This style of networking script:

1. engages the other person in the conversation with and about you
2. the person is more likely to remember you
3. the person is more likely to ask for your card

TIP: Try to get the other person to tell you what it is that they do first, be interested and ask questions. That way you might find a natural segue into your Mini-Script. But if not, they are sure to ask you what it is that you do in return.

For more brief exchanges, you can do a shortened version of this, which can actually easier to start out with as well, if you're new and not quite comfortable talking about your business yet.

'I (work with/teach/educate/inspire/support/consult/coach/etc.) with _____ (your niche) who struggle with _____(your niche's problem) _____ and who would like to _____ (your solution).

(See my own examples of this on Chapter 2.)

2. For use when speaking to groups, live or on phone, so you are always ready with your Free Taste offer.

For example, when you're leading a teleclass or live event or you're a guest on a teleclass or other live event like a workshop. You want to make sure you take advantage of the opportunity to point people to your Invite Site to sign up for your list.

Write out a Mini-Script and practice it until it feels very natural. One I get great response to is:

'I teach solo-preneurs the 6 steps to 6 figures in less than part-time hours. If you're interested in finding out how I do that, just visit aliciaforest.com for a free special report that will show you exactly how.'

Strategy 24: Utilizing Live Events (professional or personal)

To take Strategy 23 a step further…

Here are three ways to encourage people to get on your list when you meet them in person, without being pushy:

1. Put your Free Taste offering information on the back of your business card, or on whatever other materials you hand out.

Business cards are the standard pass-around marketing tool at these kind of events, but if the back of your card is blank, you're not using valuable real estate. There are several things you could add to the back of your card, and one of them is the information for your Free Taste.

Write a snappy sentence describing the benefit that the reader will get if they sign up, along with the website address of where they can subscribe.

2.   Email each person whose business card you collected within two days.

Send a brief email to each person you met, reminding them that they can sign up for your Free Taste offering at your website. Make sure you include a live link (include http://) to make it super-easy for them to click and sign up.

I sent this note to someone I met at a party:

'Dear Christine,

It was so great to meet you at Cathy's party last weekend. I enjoyed swapping the joys and trials of juggling a business and a family, and I'm really impressed with all you do while raising three children under the age of 6!
I wanted to send you the link to my free special report and ezine that I think would really help you in your marketing of your business. It's http://www.ClientAbundance.com.
Keep in touch and let me know if there are other ways I can help you.
cheers,
Alicia'

Make it personalized – make it brief.

3.   If you're a speaker at the event, or if it's your own event, have a sign-up sheet for the attendees.

Have people sign up for your list when they register for the event.

At the beginning and end of your talk, make sure you tell your audience that they can receive FREE valuable information from you if they will simply sign up on the form. Ask them for their first name and primary email address, and make note on the form what it is they will receive.

You can give each person a separate sign-up form or have one that you pass around for everyone to sign. You can also pass around a basket or bowl for people to drop their cards into to win a prize, AND to be put on your list to receive your Free Taste.

You've probably heard 'the fortune is in the follow-up' and that's exactly what this will do for you, in the form of your periodic communication with them (ezine, ecourse, etc.). If you collect their names and email addresses at the event, add them to your list with their permission, or send them a reminder email to do it themselves, your Free Taste will do the follow up for you. It will keep you on your prospects' radar screens so you'll come to mind immediately when they do need your products and services.

Strategy 25: Use a Tips Bookmark or Booklet

Stand out from the business card lot by giving away a tips bookmark or booklet instead that includes your opt-in URL.

My favorite way of creating something memorable is via a minibuk, which also allows you to insert a business card in addition to sharing your expertise: http://minibuk.com

Strategy 26: Online Networking Groups – Classic

Find 3 online networking groups and list your profile and website address that points directly to your sign-up page for your Free Taste. Visit online discussion groups at:

Yahoo: http://groups.yahoo.com
Google: http://groups.google.com
LinkedIn: www.linkedin.com

Then search the categories to find people in the niche you've chosen. Just enter the name of your niche in the search box and see what comes up.

You can use the same technique to find organizations and associations of your potential niche.

Go to www.google.com and search on 'profession name + association' (for example, 'healing arts association').

Once you discover how to access your niche, you'll want to join the conversation. Start listening, and then join in on the conversation when you can add something of value.

Remember not to sell – just educate people about what it is that you do with your mini-script. And be sure to include a direct link back to your sign-up page for your list in your email signature!

Don't forget to take advantage of PROMO days for the groups and point people to your Free Taste on your Invite Site.

Strategy 27: Online Networking Groups – Cutting Edge – Facebook

1. Join Facebook and create a profile and start building your friends list. Be sure to list the URL of your Invite Site in your profile so people know where they can sign up for your list. http://www.facebook.com

2. Once you join, search for networking groups that you can join that cater to your target market. http://www.facebook.com/groups/

   Search for your target market or keywords that your target market uses in their search for support online, and see what comes up for groups that you can consider joining.

3. Create your own group, invite people to join, and have them sign up for your list via the URL you post within the group.

The beauty of creating your own group is that you can send 'notes' to them, which is similar to when you're sending them your ezine or other information about your offerings. It's another access point to your market and helps you to deepen your relationship with them.

Strategy 28: Create Your Facebook Fan Page with an Opt-in Box

Increase the number of people who sign up for your list by creating a Facebook Fan Page.

http://snipurl.com/facebookfan

And add your opt-in box to sign up for your Free Taste to it, like this: https://www.facebook.com/aliciaforestfan/app_190322544333196

See aliciarecommends.com for a resource to help you create your fan page, quickly and very inexpensively.

Strategy 29: Twitter

Twitter is a free social networking and micro-blogging tool that allows its users to send and read other users' updates (otherwise known as tweets), which are text-based posts of up to 140 characters in length.

Updates are displayed on the user's profile page and delivered to other users who have signed up to receive them. Users can receive updates via the Twitter website, RSS, email or through other applications, like Facebook.

For list-building purposes, you can use Twitter to deepen the relationship with the people who are following you, who may not already be on your list.

Tip: You can also use Twitter in conjunction with Facebook, leveraging your networking time and effort.

Create your account with Twitter at http://www.twitter.com, then log into your account your account with Facebook and go here: http://apps.facebook.com/twitter/

Be sure to use the Twitter update tool to reach both your Twitter followers as well as your Facebook friends.

Strategy 30: 'I'm in biz' email or snail mail

Write and send a personalized email or note to your contact list about your business. Make sure you not only describe what it is that you can do for your clients, but that you also describe the kind of people you are looking to work with.

Ask your contacts to send anyone your way whom they think would benefit from your offerings. Even if your recipient doesn't know someone right away, it's likely that they will eventually and remember your note.

If you're new in business, then you want to let those people in your life who already know, like and trust you what you're up to and who your ideal clients are.

You want to make sure that your letters of introduction or update (if you've been in business for awhile) are warm and friendly. This is not a sales letter – you're simply educating your network on you and your business.

Steps:

1. Draft your letter of introduction/update
2. Make a list of everyone you know with either email or postal addresses (family, friends, colleagues, past clients, acquaintances)

3. Personalize, address and send 5 a week.
4. One week later, call those 5 people to follow-up – either by phone or in-person for a casual (non-sales-y) conversation

Strategy 31: Referrals from your Current Clients, Customers, and Centers of Influence

Periodically ask your past and current clients as well as your colleagues for referrals. Write a personalized email or note, and ask that if they know someone who might benefit from your products and/or services, to point them in the direction of your Free Taste.

Consider adding this request to your 'goodbye' packet for your clients and customers (along with request for feedback, testimonials, etc.).

Advanced Step: The most effective way of using this strategy, however, is to meet in person with your centers of influence, who are those people who come into contact with large numbers of people in your target market.

Steps:

1. Make a list of 10-20 people you know who are influential in your target market.
2. Call 3-5 of those people a week to set up a meeting, either in person over coffee (your treat) or via phone if they aren't in your geographic area.
3. During the meeting, educate them on what you do and who your ideal clients are. Ask them to refer you when appropriate. Offer to do the same for them, even if you think they might not need it.

Strategy 32: Give a Signature Talk via Teleclass

Giving a signature talk live or over the phone can be a great way to build your list with high quality subscribers.

A signature talk is a kind of speech you give over and over to various groups, and it's usually an overview or introduction of what you offer. You usually give a lot of valuable content, but you don't give away the store either.

You can use this strategy to build your list in two ways:

1. Have them sign up for your list as part of your registration process (best method).
    OR
2. On the teleseminar, offer to send notes after the call for anyone who signs up for your list. (Tip: send the notes via autoresponder.)

Strategy 33: Host a Free Open House Q&A Call

Invite your target market to a free open house Q&A call with you where they can ask you any question related to your area of expertise. In order to participate in the call, they have to register via an opt-in page that gets them on your list.

You can offer for people to email you questions for the call beforehand as well, so they will still sign up even if they can't make it live. And send a recording of the call to all who signed up afterwards too.

Tip: If you're newer in business, come to the call with 5-10 questions that you are often asked by your clients and customers so you'll be able to give valuable information as well as showcase your expertise even if your listeners are shy.

Here's a list of places where you can promote your free calls:

1. Your website

2. Your newsletter or ezine
3. Your blog
4. Your affiliates
5. Your joint venture partners
6. Your strategic alliances
7. Event calendar sites
    a. Full Calendar – http://sfbayarea.fullcalendar.com/
    b. Events Setter – http://www.eventsetter.com/
    c. Events.org – http://www.events.org/
    d. Event Brite - http://www.eventbrite.com/
8. Teleseminar/Webinar Listing Services (Free and Paid)
    a. See You On The Call – http://seeyouonthecall.com/
    b. Planet Teleclass – http://www.planetteleclass.com/
    c. Seminar Announcer – http://seminarannouncer.com/
    d. Self Growth – http://www.selfgrowth.com/
9. Twitter as a tweet
10. Facebook as a status update
11. Create a Facebook event
12. LinkedIn as a status update
13. LinkedIn on your profile
14. LinkedIn as an event
15. Other social networking sites where you are active
16. In the resource box of your articles (make sure your article is relevant to the topic)
17. Press releases
18. In your email signature
19. The listservs and discussion lists you belong to (as long as this type of promotion is allowed)
20. Forums you're active in
21. In a Pay Per Click Campaign (Facebook Ads or Google Adwords)
22. Craigslist

Strategy 34. Do Podcasts/Radio Interviews

Offer to be interviewed for a Internet radio or podcast show whose audience is your target market. Make sure you are able to give the URL of where you want people to sign up for your Free Taste as part of your interview.

To find an appropriate show, Google 'your niche + podcast' or 'your niche + radio shows.'

Two of my favorite places to find shows are:
http://www.helpareporter.com
http://www.radioguestlist.com

Your topic can be your signature talk (see #27) or on another topic that suits the interviewer. If you have two or three prepared talks that you can suggest your interview be around, you'll find it easier to secure these types of gigs and there's less work for you to prepare for them.

Tip: Researching potential interview spots is a great project to delegate to your virtual assistant.

Strategy 35. Create an Artist's Page on iTunes

To take the last strategy up a notch, create an Artist's Page on iTunes where you can list all of your podcasts that are available via subscription.

Having this page puts my business in front of thousands of iTunes subscribers. See it here: http://itunes.apple.com/ee/podcast/ creating-client-abundance/id413937418

Strategy 36. Do Speaking Gigs

This strategy is even more specific to when you are the expert, either as the speaker or guest presenter at a live event, like a workshop or conference because live speaking engagements can also be a great way to build your list.

Here are 3 more ways to collect email addresses when doing a live speaking engagement:

1. Offer a drawing/contest
    Like using the Tell-A-Friend strategy about holding a contest to increase your list numbers, at a speaking event, have your attendees give you a business card or fill out an entry form. You can offer a simple prize (book, audio program, ebook, etc) or multiple prizes.

    You want to introduce this at about the halfway point in your presentation:

    Ask your audience, 'Is this helpful? Who would like to know more about (your topic)?'

    Then follow up with your contest offer and instructions on how they can enter. Be sure to mention that you will also add them to your mailing list/newsletter.

    'Great, I'm giving away a free X so make sure you enter the drawing to be eligible. Everyone who enters will also get a free subscription to my ezine.'

    Have a volunteer or your assistant collect entries during the rest of your presentation so you can then do the drawing at the end of the presentation.

2. Ask people to submit their 'biggest question' on your topic.
    Say 'I wondered if you'd be willing to help me out with something. I want to be able to provide just what you're looking for, so if you could, take out a business card and answer this question on the back: 'What your biggest question about X?'

Have them write their answer on the back, collect them, and tell them you'll answer their questions in future newsletters.

3. Offer a copy of the notes/PowerPoint slides
    Have people sign up to receive the notes or PowerPoint slides of your presentation.

    You could also include an offer to a free 'follow-up' call after the presentation to encourage people to sign up.

    Pass around a sign-up sheet for people to give their email addresses. Make the sheet enticing by including a headline, sample from Free Taste, etc.

Strategy 37. Post comments on high-traffic sites

If you haven't already, research and join a handful of quality high traffic websites like blogs, online groups and discussion lists where your target market hangs out. Introduce yourself, listen in for a bit, and then start making valuable comments in response to the discussion that shows your expertise.

Make sure you don't sell. Your purpose here is to build relationships, and most lists will allow you a short email sig which is where you would point people to the URL for your Free Taste, or on the case of a blog, your name is linked back to your Free Taste URL.

Once you begin this process, you'll start to connect with others and make new alliances over time. I suggest you put this strategy on your marketing calendar for about 30 minutes to an hour each week. This is a subtle, but steady way to build your list numbers.

Strategy 38. Write testimonials on high-traffic sites

If you use a product or service that you absolutely love, why not write a results-based testimonial for it? Write two or three sentences about the problem you were having before you used the product or service and the great results you've gotten because of it (this is ideally how you'd like others to write your testimonials as well).

Choose three products or services you're thrilled with, write the testimonial, send it to the owner/author, adding that they are welcome to use your comments as a testimonial.

Include your name, title, business name, URL to your Free Taste, and offer to send an photo and/or to do an audio testimonial, if they'd like.

Strategy 39. Start Your Own Online Networking Group

Being a member of online networking groups is a great way to increase your list numbers. You can take that strategy to the next level by starting your own free forum within one of those networking groups. You are then not just a member of a group, but you position yourself as the host and the expert.

Start your own free discussion list for your niche through Facebook (see #21) Google Groups, LinkedIn, Yahoo Groups, etc. Then when someone in your niche is searching for like-minded colleagues, they will find your group, and you as the host and expert.

For example, I host the Coaching Zone on LinkedIn: http://tinyurl.com/coachingzone

As of this writing, there are over 20k coaches in that group that I connect with, share resources, offer advice, and yes, market to.

Every time you post to your group, make sure you have the URL in your email signature that points the members back to the page where they can sign up for your list. As your members get to know, like and trust you, they'll want to know more about you and your offerings and will likely click your link to do so.

Strategy 40. Volunteer to be a Group Moderator

If you don't want to manage your own group, an easy alternative is to volunteer to help moderate a group you're already active in or one you become active in.

Most group owners will welcome the offer of additional help to moderate. And you get to be seen as a leader in that group, which gives you more exposure and more expert status, which means more people are likely to follow your URL to sign up for your list.

Strategy 41. Ask the Expert Column

Seek out websites that are information portals for your niche, and see if they offer an 'ask the expert' section (and if they don't, you could always suggest they do). Offer your services as an expert, to answer questions from their visitors about the challenges they face.

This may be set up as a discussion list or as a column, and you are seen as the expert, as you offer your advice and wisdom to the readers. The site should allow you to post your contact information and a link back to the sign-up page for your list.

About.com is one example of an information portal site. To find others, Google 'your niche + information' or 'your niche + websites'.

Strategy 42. Write and Submit Articles

Here's why you want to implement this strategy:

1. To educate your target market about you and what you do.
2. To position you as an expert.

3.   Gives people a taste of your style, what it is that you offer, and it gives them an opportunity to get to know you a bit without risking anything.

Whether or not you consider yourself a writer, penning articles that are of value to your target market is one of the most effective ways to get your name out there and become known as an expert in your niche, attract visitors to your website, and gain new subscribers for your list.

At the end of each article you'll include a resource box, so if people want to find out more about you and your business, they have that information at their fingertips. Once someone reads your article, if they like your stuff, they will likely visit your website and sign up for your Free Taste. And writing articles is one of the fastest (and free) ways to get lots of exposure, especially if a publisher with a large list picks it up.

Here are the steps to follow:

A. Write the article or recycle one you've already written, giving it a fresh edit (it never hurts).

Write or revise an article targeted at your niche that is full of valuable content. A couple of tips: Articles can be anywhere from 300-600 words in length for the best chance of being picked up (if you have a longer article, consider chopping it in half and making it two shorter articles).

Tip: Articles with lists, steps, or mini-chunks of information seem to be the most read.

If writing an article seems difficult for you, start with putting together a Top Ten article.

Ten Steps to Writing a Top Ten Article

1.   Visit www.topten.org

This is a great website to give you ideas and samples of how a Top Ten article looks.

2.   Decide who your Top Ten is going to be written for.

To give you the best return for your investment in writing your Top Ten, it should be written for your niche. You can write a general article that applies to your entire niche, or you could choose a segment of your niche to write the article for.

3.   Decide what your Top Ten is going to be about.

To take #2 a step further, choose one issue that your niche seems to grapple with over and over, and write the article based on your solution(s) to that problem.

4.   Give it a title.

For example:

Top Ten Ways to Choose the Perfect Massage Therapist for You
Top Ten Reasons for Not Writing a Blog
Top Ten Steps to Making a Sound Business Investment
Top Ten Mistakes to Avoid When Choosing a Babysitter
Top Ten Blunders Most New Business Owners Make
Top Ten Questions to Ask Before Hiring A Virtual Assistant
Top Ten Answers to How to Design a Website
Top Ten Requirements for Traveling to Europe
Top Ten Points to Make in Any Presentation
Top Ten Hints to Keeping A Clean House Without Maid Service

5.   Create a summary paragraph about your Top Ten article.

Write a short paragraph that describes what your article is about. Three to five sentences should suffice. This will become your introductory paragraph.

6. Write down your Top Ten points.

Write down the ten points you want to make in your article. Keep each of the ten points short. For example, if your top ten article is 'Top Ten Questions to Ask Before Choosing a Massage Therapist,' your Top Ten points might be:

Point 1: Is the location of the massage therapist's office desirable?
Point 2: Does the massage therapist accept your insurance?
Point 3: Are the fees reasonable for you, if insurance is not accepted?
Point 4: Can you talk to some current clients?
Point 5: Is scheduling an appointment easy?
Point 6: Can you have your choice of a male or female therapist, if you have a preference?
Point 7: Is the environment of the therapist's office to your liking?
Point 8: Does the therapist hold certain qualifications that are important to you?
Point 9: Does the therapist have a reasonable cancellation policy?
Point 10: Know you don't have to stay with a therapist if they aren't right for you.

7. Explain each of the ten points.

Write 3 to 5 sentences to illustrate each of your ten points.

For example, Point 1: Is the location of the massage therapist's office desirable?

Think about how much time you want to spend getting to and from a potential massage therapist's office. Less is probably more desirable, or, if you're like me, I drive 30 minutes because his office is very close to the only Starbucks around where I live, so the drive is worth it to me for my weekly chai.

8.   Add your copyright.

Don't forget to protect your work by adding a copyright. At the end of each article, put a copyright notice with the date of when you first published the article. For example, copyright (or ©) 2014 Alicia M Forest, MBA.

B/9.   Write your author's resource box info.

After your copyright notice comes what's usually referred to as the 'resource box' or 'author's box.' In order for others to publish your work, ask that they include this information at the end of your article, keeping what you provide in it whole and intact. As this is standard practice, you'll find most publishers will honor this request.

Write 3-5 lines that entice people to find out more about you by providing the web address to the sign-up page for your Free Taste.

Tip: Don't send your article readers to your home page. Send them to a page set up specifically to add them to your list. For example, say 'for more articles like this, please visit www.yourezinepage.com to sign up!'

For example, one version of mine says:

Alicia Forest, MBA mentors women entrepreneurs on how to build a priority-based, highly profitable business, in less than part-time hours. Get her FREE series on how you can do this too at http:// aliciaforest.com

10.   Proofread!

Please proofread your article and your author's box. Even better, have someone else proofread it, too. It's best to have at least two sets of eyes look it over before you consider it ready to be published.

Follow these ten steps and in no time you'll have written a solid and polished article with which to market your business.

C.   Submit Your Article

Writing valuable content-rich articles for your target market and submitting them to article directories and other publishers is one of the best ways to add subscribers to your list.

For example, if you regularly write an article for your ezine, you can get a lot more mileage out of it if you submit it to article directories and other online publishing services. And making every piece you write work more than once for you is one way to work smarter and not harder. That's called leverage.

Although this is one of the most time-consuming marketing tasks, it can be made much simpler by either hiring a virtual assistant to do it for you, or by using an article submission service. The service I use is:

SubmitYourArticle.com

My link is:
http://www.submityourarticle.com/affiliates/idevaffiliate.php?id=124

There are literally hundreds of websites that offer free content for publishers who are in need of quality articles for their own publications or websites. Here are some of the best ones:
www.ezinearticles.com
www.goarticles.com
www.article-host.com
www.articlecity.com

I submit one article per week, the one I write for my ezine (so I'm leveraging my time) and I always get a slew of new subscribers when I do.

Bonus step: If you want to see even better results from submitting your articles, contact directly those publishers of ezines and websites in your niche. Google publishers of ezines in your target market and then send a query to the editor/owner about submitting an article. Present yourself as a professional and offer your article for their use, provided the resource box remains intact. Paste your article under your message (attachments can get blocked, and if the receiver doesn't know you it's unlikely they will open and read it anyway).

Make a list of 10 to 20 publishers to contact about submitting articles, and craft a friendly email to send along with your article.

For example,

Dear (name of editor),

I noticed that your ezine occasionally publishes articles from outside authors. As a reader of your ezine, I thought my article, 'name of article here' might be a good fit, and I wondered if you would consider it for publication in a future issue.

If so, please feel free to reprint the article, keeping it and the author's resource box whole and intact. If you do publish it, I'd greatly appreciate it if you'd let me know in what issue it will appear.

If you have any questions, feel free to email me at (put your email address here). However, if you do not accept articles, please let me know, and I will remove you from my publisher list.

Thank you,
Your name
Your contact info

Don't forget to paste your article right underneath your message, and not to send it as an attachment.

I also recommend that you include in your marketing plan to become a member of the Directory of Ezines. There is a membership fee, but what this does is allows you to search through hundreds of other ezines. You can search by all types of factors: topic, readership, subscriber numbers, etc. And of course, your ezine is listed as well for others to find, sign up for, or approach you for potential joint ventures/strategic alliances. Learn more here: http://www.directoryofezines.com

Commit to writing and submitting a minimum of 2-4 articles per month to steadily increase your list numbers.

Strategy 43: Be Keyword Savvy

In your articles and blog posts, choosing a set of words to use tells the search engines what your content is about, which in turn allows others to find you.

Refer to Strategy #8 to help you find the keywords your market is searching for and then use those in your articles and blog posts.

You want to write naturally and insert keywords sparingly yet prominently. Your keywords can be included in the title of your post as well as the first paragraph of your post, then again in a few of your subheadings.

A sprinkle of keywords in your writing can attract more traffic to your site which will lead to more subscribers to your list.

Strategy 44: Leverage Amazon's Market Reach by Writing Reviews

There are 3 subtle and secret ways for building your list - and by default make money - using Amazon's power:

1. Writing reviews
2. Creating a 'So, you'd like to…' guide
3. Creating Listmania lists

Amazon.com gets a lot of very focused, quality traffic. By posting reviews, Listmania lists, and So, you'd like to… guides, you put yourself in the 'way' of all of that traffic.

When someone reads your review, your list, or your guide and clicks on your URL to visit your site, you will add subscribers to your list.

1. Write a review of 3 books central to your theme/niche

To write a review, choose 3 of your favorite books or products that you've personally used that your niche would also be interested in and search for them on Amazon.

Click on the 'Write a Review' link and you're off. It doesn't have to be long. In fact, the shorter it is (one or two 3-5 sentence paragraphs), the more likely it will be read.

Strategy 45: Leverage Amazon's Reach with a "So, you'd like to…" Guide

The easy way to create a 'So you'd like to…' guide is to search for books and the link will come up on the sidebar, or create it from your profile.

One of the things we're trying to accomplish as business owners is to be viewed as an expert on what it is that we're offering to our niche. A fantastic way to do this is to create a 'So, you'd like to…' guide at Amazon where you can share your advice with others.

Your guide will appear on Your Profile and other places on the site.

These guides are a way for you to help other people find all the items and information they might need for something they are interested in.

As you create your guide, keep in mind that you needn't have purchased these items at Amazon.com. Each So You'd Like to… guide can cover all sorts of topics, and can be as specific or as general as you'd like.

You can include any item from the Amazon.com store that has a 10-digit ASIN or an International Standard Book Number (ISBN). An ASIN or ISBN is a unique number used to identify each item in the Amazon. com store. These unique item numbers are displayed on the product information page for each item.

Go ahead and create a So You'd Like to… guide. It's free, easy, and fun. Simply click the 'Write a So You'd Like to… guide' link on Your Amazon Home to start.

Strategy 46: Leverage Amazon's Reach with a Listmania list

Listmania lists include products you find of value. For example, a short list of books you always refer to in reference to your business.

You needn't have purchased them from Amazon to create a Listmania list, and you can create pretty much any category you'd like.

Your list helps other people in their search for information, which makes you the expert.

You can create a list by following a link to 'Create Your Own List' on an existing Listmania list. Or an easy way to create a Listmania list at Amazon is to search for any book, and on the right hand side of page, you will see words 'Listmania' 'Add your list'. Just click on 'Add your list' and go from there. If you create a profile for yourself, you can start your list from that page as well.

Lists you create will appear on your profile. Amazon may also provide a link to your lists on the search results page of searches related to the items in your list. People can check out your other recommendations by clicking your name at the top of your list – this will take them to your profile.

Strategy 47: Offer a Free Teleseminar Series Featuring Experts (with a twist)

To take Strategy #12: Interview with Experts to an advanced level, this is a great strategy to consider to build a relationship with your colleagues, to increase your credibility and name recognition, as well as to quickly increase your list numbers.

An 'Expert' series can be as simple as 3 or 4 interviews over the course of a few weeks, or as long as 12 speakers over the course of as many weeks, or 10 speakers in 5 days (often referred to as a "telesummit"). Your options are really limitless but the format is the same regardless of the number of experts you interview. (See Strategy #12 for details on how to secure experts for your series.)

Your series should be targeted to your market, with the topics that each expert will be speaking about centered around a general theme that would be of interest to both your list as well as your experts' list.

The twist is to offer the series for free, with an optional upgrade package. Basically, once someone registers for the series, they are then directed to a web page where they can "upgrade" their registration to receive the audio recordings of the event and possibly transcripts as well for a fee.

Offering your experts a commission on any registrant who upgrades via their unique affiliate link, as well as the opportunity to promote something of their own at the end of their interview, will result in an increase in list numbers as well as an increase in income for both of you.

Strategy 48: Host a Free Video Summit

Take the idea of a telesummit up a notch by hosting a video summit instead. This format requires a bit more technology-wise, and I'd recommend having help to pull it off successfully, whether that's a tech-savvy virtual assistant or a company who provides this kind of service.

Just a few reasons to host a video summit include higher perceived value, higher conversion rates, and higher list numbers for future money-making opportunities.

Strategy 49: Offer a Free Video Tips Series

While it's a great idea to do a video tips series leading up to a paid offer, you can utilize this strategy to attract people to sign up for your list as well. Offering free valuable content in this format is one of the most effective strategies working online today.

Successful video tip series are short (2-3 minutes each) and focuses on a problem that your market would 'pay anything, do anything' to solve.

You could create your series and offer as your Free Taste or to infuse your list with new subscribers a couple of times a year.

Strategy 50. Host Your Own Web TV Show

If you'd rather speak than write to show your expert status, and you're comfortable in front of the camera, then consider hosting your own web TV show.

You can start simply with your own YouTube channel or kick it up a notch by allowing your viewers to interact live with you via your own LiveStream channel.

To build your list, simply ask your viewers to sign up for your list to be alerted to new episodes.

Strategy 51. Create a Viral Movie

Creating a viral movie is another way of using online video to increase your list numbers. Your goal with your movie is to connect with your viewers on an emotional level, and engage them enough so they sign up for your list.

At the end of the movie, give the URL where your viewers only option is to sign up for you list. Or if you have the movie playing on a dedicated page on your website, put your opt-in box right below it to make it super-simple for someone to sign up right away.

If you need help in creating your viral movie, I recommend MindMovies. This software is meant for creating your own affirmation movies, which I recommend as well, but you can create a viral movie to promote your business, too (and it's a lot less expensive than having someone create it for you).

My link is:
http://www.mindmovies.com/?10080

Once your movie is complete, post it to the most popular video sharing sites, as well on its own web page with an opt-in box:

- youtube.com
- video.google.com
- video.yahoo.com
- revver.com
- veoh.com
- blip.tv
- viddler.com
- vimeo.com

Strategy 52. Create a Viral eBook

Much like a viral movie, a viral ebook can help increase your list numbers as well as increase your reach (and good karma!) into your target market.

The process goes like this:

1. Create a free ebook to give away.

Your free ebook doesn't have to be longer than 10 pages to be effective. Make sure it's focused on solving a problem that your target market in general struggles with, and it will get passed around (that's what makes it viral).

2. Make an offer

In your ebook, you want to be sure to make an offer to the reader. Your offer should be something of value that gives more by way of solutions to their problems that you are touching upon in your ebook. In order to take advantage of your offer, however, they are required to sign up for your list.

For tracking purposes, be sure to use a tracking link for your offer so you know which subscribers are coming from your ebook.

3. Give permission to pass it on

In your ebook, be sure to make it clear that your reader has your permission to pass on the ebook, as long as it remains unchanged and intact.

4. Track your results

As your ebook gets passed along, you can track your results via the tracking links and tweak as necessary.

Strategy 53. Write Your Manifesto and Go Viral with it

Much like a viral movie and viral ebook can help increase your list numbers as well as increase your reach (and good karma!) into your target market, a manifesto takes that one step further.

According to Andrea Lee (one of my first coaches), there are three basic parts to a manifesto:

1. Be passionate
2. Be succinct and direct
3. Leave the reader with a charge

Because a manifesto has an inherently viral nature it's a great list-building tool.

What I personally like about writing your manifesto is that those who resonate with it and sign up for your list to hear more from you are usually your most responsive subscribers to your offers.

Here are your steps:

1. Write your manifesto
   Your manifesto can be short and sweet – even 5 points that you passionately believe in with a few sentences underneath is enough.

2. Include your opt-in URL
   Be sure to add the URL for people who resonate with your manifesto to sign up for your list, and then...

3. Offer it with no opt-in required
   Send your manifesto to your current lists and networks with no obligation to opt-in to receive it.

4. Give permission to pass it on
   In your manifesto, be sure to make it clear that your reader has your permission to pass it on, as long as it remains unchanged and intact.

Strategy 54. Write and Self-Publish a Print Book

One of the fastest ways to open the flow of attention and reach into your market is via a print book, which can in turn lead to loads of new subscribers.

You can use your print book to secure radio and TV interviews and invite listeners and viewers to visit a mini-site where they can receive a free chapter of your book when they opt-in to your list.

Strategy 55. Press Releases

Test each offer and activity you're doing in your business to see if it's newsworthy. If it is, then submit a press release at services such as PRWeb or BusinessWire. You will likely get a surge of new subscribers, as well as a number of inbound links. For templates on how to write a press release, visit:

www.prnewswire.com
www.prweb.com
www.press-release-writing.com/press-release-template/
www.publicityinsider.com/release.asp

Strategy 56. Pay for Advertising (including PPC)

1. Advertise in trade publications, associations and other newsletters applicable to your target market.

Look for publications that accept advertising, and follow the instructions to inquire about their advertising policies and rates.

You want to know how many subscribers they have on their list, where your ad will be placed in the publication, how many issues you will be in and the type of ad allowed (text-only or graphics).

Costs on advertising can vary depending on the market and the size of their list. Be sure to track any paid advertising to make sure that you get an appropriate return on your investment.

As you're researching publications in your target market, be on the lookout for those that accept advertising. If possible, connect with a current advertiser or two and ask them what their return on investment has been in that publication.

Once you decide where to advertise, run your ad for at least three consecutive issues for the best results. A common mistake that business owners make is to only run an ad once, but remember that people need to see your message multiple times before it will even register, so a minimum of three times to make an accurate assessment if the ROI is worthwhile is best.

2.   Another form of paying for advertising is doing a Pay-Per-Click campaign like Google Adwords or Facebook Ads. PPC is such a gift to the entrepreneur. There's nothing quite like being able to advertise for pennies and then only for those visitors who find your site through your PPC Ad. You have complete control over your campaign, so you never have to worry about exceeding your budget, and that budget can be very small and still be very effective.

You can create a PPC campaign for a very small investment, and because you have complete control over your budget, you can set it for whatever amount you feel comfortable with. It's very difficult to get to the top of the 'organic' search results (on the left side of the search results page) but can be very easy to get on the first page of results with a PPC, bringing targeted traffic to you. Again, the best part is you only pay when someone clicks your ad that takes them to your website.

Visit http://adwords.google.com and take a tour of what Adwords can do for you. Do the same on Facebook: http://www.facebook.com/home.php?#/advertising/

Strategy 57. Add Direct Mail by Renting/Buy a Mailing List and Send a Simple Postcard

When you're very clear on your target market, consider buying or renting a mailing list made up of those in your target market that you can reach via postal mail.

Different mailing list providers have different ways and methods of working, so be sure to do some research before you commit to any one broker.

To get you started, one company I've found to have great information and free search function is: http://www.nextmark.com/

Once you've received your list, keep it simple by sending them a postcard invite to sign up for your list, using the components we cover in the beginning of this book for creating a compelling Invite Site and Free Taste.

Your Free Taste – Part II: Your Ezine

Having an online ezine/newsletter is one of the easiest ways to keep in contact with your niche. Not only will you be able to tell your subscribers about any new products or services you've created (and offering them a discount for being subscribers makes them feel special and even more a part of your online community), as well as about any live program and events you'll be holding, but you'll also be able to connect with them on a personal level, by sharing with them a bit about your life as well, deepening the relationship for even better business building.

Here are ten very good reasons why you should offer an ezine (originally cited by Ali Brown, once known as the Ezine Queen):

1. It is one of the easiest and most effective ways to promote your products, programs and services.
2. It helps to establish you as an expert in your niche.
3. It helps you stay in front of your niche without feeling pushy (since they opt-in to be a subscriber) on a consistent basis.
4. If your content has value, it will spread and your business will become known.
5. It's one way to capture the email addresses of your website visitors to build your list.
6. It's one of the best low-cost ways to stop being a secret!
7. It's the easiest way to create a membership website by converting your subscribers to members.
8. You can compile the 'best of the best' information in your niche and offer it in one place – your ezine – which encourages people to return to you over and over for information that they then don't have to search elsewhere for.
9. You can offer advertising space and add to your revenue stream.
10. You can start today!

Tip: You can send your ezine out once a week, twice a month, or once a month. I usually recommend sending it at least twice a month – otherwise it's going to take a longer period of time to convert your subscribers into buyers.

Common marketing knowledge is that it takes anywhere from 5-12 times for a prospective client to buy. That means you have to get your message in front of them at least that many times (particularly if you are new to them or you haven't been referred by a trusted source) before they will consider making a purchase. An ezine is an easy way to do this, without feeling like you're being pushy, particularly because your subscribers have asked to receive your information by way of subscribing to your publication.

But there is a KEY POINT to make here: Your ezine's content MUST have value for your readers. If it doesn't have value, it doesn't get read or recommended, so it doesn't grow, and neither does your business. In fact, the more value you can give in your newsletter, the more buzz will be created around it, the more it will get passed around, the more potential clients will visit your site to subscribe, and the more they will eventually become part of your paying community.

An ezine is one of the seeds that you will sow over time, as you build trust and credibility with your readers, so keep at it, and you will soon see new clients showing up to work with you and new customers buying your products and joining your programs.

Your first issue(s) doesn't have to be more than a text message with a single tip, so no excuses. If that's where you're at, great – go for it. Start there and let it evolve with you. Your readers will really connect with you for coming as you are.

Deliver Your Ezine

Now that you've written your first issue, you need a delivery system for it (even if you don't have more than a handful of subscribers at the moment). You can deliver your ezine the same way you've chosen to deliver autoresponders, if you're using them at this point (and if you aren't, you will eventually).

So, whatever list service you're using is how you'll deliver your ezine, since that is where your subscribers' emails are housed.

Here are the most popular list services providers:
Aweber: http://snipurl.com/aweberautoresponders
1ShoppingCart: http://snipurl.com/shoppingcart1

If you're using Aweber, you simply use the Broadcast function under the 'messages' tab and follow the same steps you did for sending autoresponder messages. The list that you've started building from the people who signed up to receive your Free Taste is the same list you'll be sending your ezine to (make sure you've told them that when they sign up for your Free Taste that they will also get your ezine).

You'll be able to queue your ezine to be broadcast to your list whenever you want. So, for example, if you're going on vacation, but still want your issue to go out to your list while you're away, you can write it ahead of time and choose the date and time of delivery that you want.

Take Your Ezine to the Next Level

Once you've got a handful of issues under your belt, consider taking your ezine up a notch. Writing a regular ezine/newsletter can sometimes feel a bit cumbersome. So if you're putting in the time and effort to give your readers valuable content, consider implementing at least a few of these strategies to help your efforts pay off in profits.

Here are 4 ways to help your ezine make you more money:

1. Self-promote

Besides giving valuable content in each issue of your ezine, don't forget to add a little self-promotion as well. After all, your ezine is one of your best marketing tools, and you want to make sure that you're letting your subscribers know what products, programs and services you have available for them.

Tip: Aim for 80% free valuable content and 20% promotions. If that feels like too much for your market, shoot for at least 10% promotions and work up to 25%-30% as your list (and their tolerance for promotions) grows.

It's best to do this in a separate section of your ezine, instead of in the copy of the article you write for your readers. A short blurb about you and what you offer, as well as a bit about one of your products, programs and services with a link to more information is all you really need to do.

Tip: Consider adding one or two short testimonials from your clients/ customers who are raving fans.

Tip: Depending on the method through which you are publishing your ezine, you can track how many times your links are clicked on, which gives you valuable market research information about what your readers are interested in finding out more about.

2. Give options

There are likely many people who would like to hire you one-on-one but that option doesn't fit into their budget just yet. If you offer them other options, and promote those offerings in your ezine, you'll turn some of those prospects into paying customers and most likely future clients.

For example, if you coach or consult one-on-one, consider offering a group coaching program with a price point that would be much more accessible than your private fees would be. Or take your knowledge and package it into an information product, like a series of teleseminars, or an ecourse, and price them reasonably. Then promote these offers in your ezine.

3.   Offer specials

Your readers may find the content of your free ezine valuable and would really like more, but they might need a bit of encouragement to buy from you. So give your subscribers a special discount on something you offer, with a time limit for purchasing (which really does encourage people to 'act now').

For example, offer a 2-for-1 deal on your ebooks, or 20% off one of your programs if they register within a week. This strategy will move some of your readers from the 'free' part of your M&P Funnel into the 'fee' part of your Funnel, which is exactly what you want.

4.   Offer recommendations

I get so many questions about the services I use in my business that I used to periodically give recommendations in my ezine, and now I have a dedicated page for them that I point readers to at aliciarecommends. com. These products and services are ones I truly believe are of high quality, because I have used them personally or because they come highly recommended to me by my colleagues. Some of these I am a reseller of (an affiliate), meaning I make a small commission on every referral I make, but all of them are products and services I know would be of value to my subscribers.

Don't forget that your number one priority with your ezine is to provide valuable content for your subscribers. And remember to proportion 20%

of your content with promoting you and your offerings, and you will be working smarter and not harder.

Also remember that with each issue you put out, you are building trust and rapport with your list, becoming known as an expert in your niche, and gaining lots of exposure (especially if you submit your ezine articles to article submission services as we covered earlier), all of which are important to the overall success of your business.

STEP 6

Productize Your Services

Now that you've created your Free Taste and a place to offer it on your Invite Site, and you're working diligently on building that critical-to-your-6-figure-success email list of potential clients and customers, let's move on to 'productizing' your services to create leveraged streams of income for you.

There's more to business than one-on-one sessions, and creating and offering products is the best way to leverage your time and talent. Simply put, you'll help more people AND make more money – so it's a win-win.

Your first for-fee product should fall into the first level of your Funnel, with a price point between $1 - $50.

You've essentially created your first product with your Free Taste. Now it's time to create your first for-fee product, which will obviously be meatier and more complex than your Free Taste, but it doesn't have to be a multi-media product either.

Just like with the Free Taste, I suggest creating your first for-fee product based on your strengths. For example, if you like to write, an ebook or ecourse would be a good offering for you. If you prefer to talk, create an audio product or offer a teleseminar. These are the most common and most profitable products to offer in the first level of your Funnel.

You'll follow the same process for creating and delivering your for-fee products as you did for creating your Free Taste (except that you'll be accepting payments this time, which we'll cover later in this chapter).

Let's review the steps to develop your for-fee product, as I'm sure by now you've got a slew of ideas written down in your notebook, so choose your favorite and get to work.

Remember the Online Business Breakthrough Formula:

Your Unique Message + Your Niche + Your Niche's Problem + Your Solution Packaged = Your Profitable Product/Program/Service (= new income stream)

Review Step 3 for detailed information on creating your for-fee offering, but here is the simple formula in a nutshell:

1. Choose a problem that your niche wants solved.
2. Create the solution to that problem.
3. Package your solution and set it up for delivery.
4. Offer your solution to your niche for a fee.

Tip: For support and cheering on in developing products, programs, and services for your Funnel, be sure to join the Studio with your special invitation found at the end of this book.

Accepting Payments

Once you've got your first for-fee product created, and you've set it up for delivery, you'll need to set up how people will pay for it. To get started, PayPal is a viable and easy-to-use option.

If you want something with more bells and whistles, you can get a shopping cart system (if you haven't invested in one already). But remember that you need a merchant account in order to make this work. A merchant account is an account with a bank that processes credit card transactions for you for a small percentage of each transaction. PayPal usually has the lowest fees, but if you're using another shopping cart system (where it is a seamless transaction, no third-party involvement (like with PayPal)), you'll need to apply for and get approved for a merchant account first. If you decide to go this route, you might want to shop around for the best fees.

Tip: I use and recommend Practice Pay Solutions at www. practicepaysolutions.com for a merchant account, and InfusionSoft for a shopping cart. Before using InfusionSoft, I used and still recommend 1ShoppingCart at http://snipurl.com/shoppingcart1

For your first for-fee product, PayPal is a great place to start. Then once you start making about $1000 a month in sales you can start looking at adding a merchant account and private shopping cart to your business.

Once your first product is ready, go to www.paypal.com and set up your account, or set up your shopping cart with your new product, following the instructions for your chosen system.

Write Your Sales Page for Your For-Fee Product

Once you have your for-fee product ready to go, you'll need to write the copy for the sales page.

Often when I take a look at my client's websites to see how they have their products or services positioned, I find that they usually have one page devoted to their offerings, with a brief description and the fee associated with each. And yes, it's one page I recommend you have as part of your website. But you also need to have a separate sales page for each product or service you are providing to convert the most prospects into buyers and to get more traffic from the search engines.

You don't have to be a professional copywriter to write good sales copy. Below is the outline of what elements to include for writing a sales letter that engages your prospect so they are more likely to buy.

1. Have a strong headline.

This first thing that your potential buyers will read is your headline, and if it's not compelling enough, they won't read any further. You have to grab them right away, and that usually means touching them emotionally and relating to the pain they are feeling at the moment.

To get your creative juices flowing, start with this headline: 'How to _____ so you can _____.'

Fill in the blanks with your proposition. For example, 'How to Sell Your Products Online So You Can Make Money While You Sleep.' As you write your sales copy, your headline will likely change to be a bit more compelling. You'll get ideas and start coming up with words and phrases that are unique and specific to your offering.

Tip: It's important that the second part of your headline tell what benefit your potential buyer will enjoy to keep them reading.

2. Talk about the challenge your prospect is struggling with, especially if it is one you've also struggled with and have overcome.

If you touch upon your potential buyers' pain, they will feel that you understand where they're at and they will feel more compelled to keep reading to see if you have the potential to solve their problem.

If you've struggled with the same issue and have successfully overcome it, even better. Your solution, then, will be more credible to your potential client and customer.

3. Introduce yourself.

Your prospect will want to know who you are and why you're qualified to offer your product or service. Give them a sense of your experience and knowledge, and make them feel that you know what you're talking about (because you do!).

Adding a photo (and even audio or video) is a great way to connect with your prospect because it makes you more 'real' to them, which is particularly important online. It helps to build trust that there is a person 'behind the curtain,' and you know by now that people only buy things from people they know, like and trust.

4. Use sub-headlines.

As you write your sales copy, break up everything your prospect will get in easy to digest chunks. Use sub-heads as mini-headlines to keep your reader engaged. This is particularly important if you are writing a longer sales letter, as most people will just skim it. So pull out, bold, make bigger, etc. any copy that highlights the benefits the prospect will get from your offering. Don't forget to use an easy to read font, and use plenty of white space to keep your potential buyer reading.

5. List the benefits of your products.

Don't put your entire table of contents in your sales letter. Turn each into an enticing reason to buy.

For example, if you are selling an ebook on dealing with the sleep deprivation that comes with a newborn, write something like, 'You'll learn the 5 secrets to getting more sleep without feeling guilty.'

6. Use testimonials.

Pepper testimonials from previous buyers throughout your sales page, listing their full name (no initials) and website URL or city and state, whichever is appropriate. If this is a new product that you don't have testimonials for yet, consider offering a few review copies, or use testimonials from other products and services you've offered (just be clear what the testimonial is for). Add your raving fan's photo and audio or video for more impact.

7. Explain your price.

Give your readers a reason why you've priced your product as you have. If you make a good case and it makes sense to them, they are that much more likely to buy.

Also, show the value they'll get from your offering. For example, if you are offering a group coaching program, compare the cost of that program to your private one-on-one fees.

8. Offer some complementary bonuses.

Give away some great bonuses with your product. Ones that have a high perceived value and that are also created by you are best, but offering bonuses from colleagues whose offering complement yours is also a great strategy.

9. Offer a guarantee.

Eliminate the risk for your prospect by giving an unconditional, no-questions-asked guarantee. Most people won't take you up on it, but knowing it's there if they need to invoke it goes far in removing any hesitancy about buying. This is especially true for a higher ticket item.

10. Create scarcity to increase sales.

Offer your product or service with a special limited time offer. But really do make it limited – don't use one of those annoying scripts that changes the date on your sales page, but your offer never actually changes. If you say you're going to raise your price after a certain date, then make sure you raise your price (and that doesn't mean you can't have a sale at a later date).

11.   Have a clear call to action.

Tell your prospect exactly what they need to do next. Walk them through the buying process, step-by-step. Make your 'buy now' button prominent, with something like 'Click the BUY NOW button below to place your order now' with it.

Tip: Place your order link at the top and a few times throughout your sales page so whenever someone decides they are ready to buy, you've made it easy for them. Say something like, 'Ready to buy now? Great! Just click the BUY NOW button below.'

12.   Add a PS or two.

Don't you almost always read the PS in a letter, even if you haven't read another word of it? Use this valuable add-on to encourage your prospects to act immediately.

Tip: The PS is the second most read part of a sales page, the headline being the first. Make sure you use both well.

13.   Add your contact info.

Don't forget to add your contact information so that if someone has a question (and they will!) they can easily contact you for an answer. Listing your email address and a phone number also makes you seem more legitimate to your prospect, even if they don't need to contact you right then.

14. Make your sales page an Invite Site.

The one thing you don't want to do is allow your prospects to click away from your sales page, even if it's to look at some of your other offerings. So don't create your sales page as just another web page within your website, with all the navigation intact. Create a separate page, focused only on the product, program or service you're offering.

Tip: It's often a good idea to ask your sales page visitors to sign up for your list, if they aren't already on it. You can add your sign-up form for your Free Taste to your sales page, but just make sure it's set off in some way, like in a PS or a 'By the way,…' box and have it open in a new window, or via a pop-up.

One of the best and easiest ways to write good copy is to model (not copy) other good copy. Review the sales pages of other products and service that you've personally invested in, and/or ones that sell a similar item that you are offering. Then write your sales copy, using the others as models, while implementing the techniques listed in this step.

For your first for-fee product, which should be priced anywhere from $1 to $50, you don't need a really long sales letter. If you make sure you've implemented the techniques in this step, a sales page of no more than 3-5 pages should suffice.

Create Your Next Product

Once you've launched your first for-fee product (congratulations!), I'm sure you'll be fired up to get working on your next one.

But how do you decide which product to create next?

Take a look at your Funnel and identify any holes. Right now, you should have your Free Taste at the top and one for-fee product in the first level at the $1-$50 price point. You should also have your one-on-one services at the bottom of your Funnel, at the highest price point.

Now you have a choice. You can develop another product for the first level, which will be easier the second time around, and you will probably get it to your market faster than a higher ticket item.

Or you can start working on the next level of the Funnel and create something to offer in the $51-$200 level. It's up to you. An easy way to create a product for the next price point is to add some additional content and components to your level 1 product.

For example, if you created an ebook for $27, you could add some meatier content and a few audio downloads and sell it as a course for $87. Or you could take that same ebook, break it into learnable chunks of information and offer a series of teleclasses for $127. Your options really are endless.

In the meantime, don't forget to keep marketing your first product. Like your Free Taste, your lower priced product will bring in more buyers, of whom a certain percentage will move down the Funnel to the next higher priced level.

And that's it…! Now you just rinse and repeat. Anytime you want to create something new, go back to the Online Business Breakthrough Marketing & Product Formula: ask your niche what it wants, then create it and offer it to them. It's a profitable formula every time.

BONUS STEP: WHAT NEXT?

So, what's next for you…? Here are my thoughts:

1. **Continue to fill in your Online Business Breakthrough Marketing & Product Funnel,** one level at a time. I know it's hard not to jump to the higher ticket levels, but hold yourself back long enough to create smaller and less expensive offerings to fill in the top few levels first. If you do that, not only will you attract more clients and make more sales, you'll also make creating your larger, more complex offerings that much easier because you'll have done a good portion of the work already. Meanwhile, you'll enjoy some consistent cash flow from your smaller offerings as long as you consistently market them to your list(s).

2. **Continue to build your list** by implementing 6-8 of the 50+ strategies I gave you to attract your ideal clients and customers. The larger your list, the more profit potential it has. Make 1000 subscribers your first goal. Once you reach 1000 people, it's a tipping point, where you'll start to see and enjoy a steady flow of cash (again, as long as you continue to consistently market). Your next tipping point after 1000 is 3000, which should move you into a whole new tax bracket. And it's upwards from there. The first 1000 will seem the hardest to get and take the longest to reach (although not always), but after that, it snowballs, and hitting 3000 doesn't seem nearly as out of reach as you're thinking right now.

3. **Keep learning!** Learn to write sales copy, learn techniques to launch your products and programs for higher sales, learn how to make

changes to your website, learn the latest online marketing strategies, hire a coach, join a group coaching program, and use your special invitation to join the Studio to help you with all of this and more.

4. **Start building relationships with people in your niche with whom you'd like to joint venture.** Creating a new product can be easier with two people putting forth the effort, and you can market that product to both your lists, making it a win-win all around.

5. **Consider speaking and holding live events.** Speaking and holding live events will help build your confidence and get you out from behind your desk and engaged on a whole other level with the people whose problems you want to help solve. It helps you stay in touch with what's keeping them up at night so you can get ideas for new offerings, and it's also is a great way to build your list and bring in some additional income.

6. **Keep up with new technologies.** Video, evergreen webinars, Pinterest, and Livestream events are hot right now and aren't going away anytime soon, and a lot of people still don't know much about utilizing these in their business yet. Stay ahead of the curve to build your expertise in your niche. I'll keep you updated in my ezine as well.

7. **Have fun!** Don't get so caught up in your business that you forget to live the rest of your life. I know when you're passionate about something and excited about plowing ahead, it's very easy to be at your desk for hours on end. But you'll be a much happier and productive person if you take regularly scheduled breaks – like on the weekends, and on vacation. So don't work so hard that you forget to enjoy why you went into business for yourself in the first place, ok?

BONUS CHAPTER: HIRE HELP

I'm often asked 'what's the one thing you wish you had done differently when you started your business?' My answer is always that I wish I had hired help sooner.

Maybe you're like I was and you do everything yourself when it comes to running your business. Or maybe you find it difficult to delegate to others, at least sometimes. Or maybe you think you don't have the money to hire help. Well, I'm going to show you how hiring help can help increase your bottom line dramatically.

Not delegating is one of the major hurdles my private clients seem to struggle with. They are doing everything themselves and are so busy with the administrative tasks that they have little time to devote to their 'genius' work - developing products and services for their niche and working directly with their clients. Once they've hired help, either a virtual assistant or an in-office assistant, and move through the growing pains of delegating and trusting that the work will get done (and might even get done faster and better than they could do it themselves), I can always sense a feeling of freedom and excitement as the space opens up for them to work on the things that are really creative and inspiring to them, instead of dealing with invoices or fixing a glitch with their web page. And very soon after, their business really starts to move forward because they have the time and focus to dedicate to increasing their signature line of products, programs and services, which, of course, translates into more profits.

There are many ways that you can work with an assistant. You can hire someone on an hourly basis, or hire someone on a monthly retainer, which is often less expensive. You can hire someone for a single project only or you could hire someone fulltime to work in your office with you. Think about which of these scenarios might work best for you.

If you hire someone as an employee, remember to check with your accountant about filing the appropriate paperwork. The beauty of working with a freelancer, independent contractor or virtual assistant is that they cover their own overhead, including any insurance needs.

Here are 10 ways you can use an assistant:

1. submitting your articles to hundreds of submission sites
2. handling registrations for your teleclasses/workshops
3. proofing and formatting your written material
4. creating graphics for your products
5. maintaining your website
6. inputting any necessary updates to your products/programs/ services
7. as a sounding board for new ideas
8. responding to your customer/client/jv inquiries
9. bookkeeping
10. packaging and shipping your products

If you can't quite see how an assistant could help you deal with all the time-suckers in your business, keep a log of your business activities for a week, including how long each task takes you to complete. Then at then end of the week, review it and circle all the tasks that an assistant can help you with (there should be quite a few). Consider the number of hours those things have taken you to accomplish, and decide if the $10-$50 an hour for an assistant would be worth the investment. Statistics tell us that your bottom line could increase as much as 40% once you hire help - now that's a pretty good return on investment, isn't it? (My own revenues nearly doubled after I hired my first virtual assistant.)

And if you still think you can't afford to hire someone, then start asking around in your network for someone who would be interested in an exchange of services, or for an intern or apprentice.

Check aliciarecommends.com for VA recommendations or ask your colleagues who are happy with their own VAs to see if any of their assistants are looking for additional clients.

So before you burn out and lose the passion for owning your own business that you started off with, hire someone to help you. You'll reach more people with your message and make more money at the same time. Start small and add hours as you feel comfortable and for what you find necessary. You'll never regret it and you'll never go back to being a lone ranger – that I know for sure.

EPILOGUE

Summer 1970 to today...

I was just three months old when I was christened in Lake Winnipesaukee in New Hampshire. For 20+ summers, I reveled in this peaceful escape, from the day after school ended in June until the day before school began each September. The lake was the place where I was the happiest, and as I grew older and went on to college and then to work for someone else after graduation, then got married, and then went into business for myself, I always returned to the lake each summer – if only for a week here and there, or a long weekend or two. But one of my dreams was to spend the entire summer at the lake again, like I did growing up, and in particular for James and me to share that experience with our daughter Chloe and son Jack.

On June 30, 2006, my dream became my reality. On that date, my family and I moved into a cozy yet beautiful lakefront cottage for the summer. It really was a dream come true, and it would not have been possible were it not for the business I've created. As I write this epilogue from the dock at that same cottage, this is our ninth summer here, where we are spending 11 weeks together as a family. It brings tears of gratitude to my eyes to write that.

I share this deeply personal dream with you as a real-life example of what following the steps, strategies, and model in this book can do for you and your business. Whatever your dream is, you CAN attain it.

You will have to put in some effort. You will have to do some of what I call 'thirsty work' – the kind that feels really good once you're done and you can sit back and enjoy a cold drink.

What I've shared with you is not a get-rich-quick scheme. What it is, is a real-world, real-people proven system that works. It's worked for me and for thousands of other entrepreneurs like me – and like you.

You will create wealth for yourself and a legacy for your family if you follow the steps I've outlined for you in this book. Then it's a matter of staying nimble, ahead of the curve, and continuing to get mentoring and coaching to support you in developing your dream business.

And now, I'd like to invite you to do something...

If you're read this book through, take a pen and paper and write the most Vivid Vision of your future that you can imagine.

There are just 3 rules to follow when you do this exercise:

1. Do not censor yourself. Just write freely, without editing your thoughts.
2. Do not limit yourself. You do not need to know how you are going to achieve all that you want and desire.
3. Have fun!

Once you've written your Vivid Vision, send it to me at alicia@aliciaforest. com. I can't promise that I will respond to it personally, but know that it will be read. And know also that by doing this exercise, you've put your intentions out to the Universe of exactly what it is that you want. This simple act allows the Universe to then align itself to bring you everything you've written down. You don't even need to believe this to be true.

You just need to be open to receiving it.

Remember,

'What you are seeking, is seeking you.'
- Wayne Dyer

Cheers to your success!
~ A

HOW TO REACH US

If you'd like more information about how Alicia Forest can help you, please visit http://www.AliciaForest.com. There you'll find information on:

- The 21 Easy & Essential Steps to Online Success System™
- List-Building Secrets home-study program
- Launch Logistics home-study program
- Alicia's Group Coaching Programs
- VIP Mentoring with Alicia
- Annual Online Business Breakthrough Workshop
- And much more…

If you want to connect with Alicia and her team today, just send an email to support@aliciaforest.com and we'll get back to you shortly.

Alicia is available for speaking engagements, either virtual (via teleseminar, webinar or video) or in-person. Her most popular talk is her *6 Simple Steps to a 6 Figure Solo Business*, her 60-minute signature talk that walks her audience through the exact steps they need to take to build a 6-figure income using the power of the Internet with integrity and authenticity.

For availability, please email support@aliciaforest.com

ABOUT ALICIA

Alicia Forest, MBA, has devoted over a decade of her professional life to achieving excellence in entrepreneurship. She brings her years of hands-on experience to help struggling entrepreneurs re-design their business into one that is priority-based and highly profitable, in less than part-time hours.

With her signature spirited style, youthful energy and exceptional skills as a catalyst and educator, Alicia Forest is without question the go-to girl for guidance for online business owners.

Alicia's resume reads like a biography of a born entrepreneur. From the beginning of her career when she was 12 years old selling handmade ribbon barrettes to her recent recognition as the 'Business Breakthrough Mentor', Alicia has been completely devoted to the art of building a successful business based on the passionate serving of others.

Over the years, Alicia has worked with a who's who of the industry and has continuously developed, fine-tuned and broadened her skills as an alchemist, educator and business owner.

Since 2001, Alicia regularly meets with clients from around the world to educate and inspire them to marry money and meaning in their business. Many of those clients create 6-figure incomes as a direct result of working privately with Alicia.

Alicia has been featured in several publications including Entrepreneur. com, Smart Confident Woman Magazine, Artella, Holistic Business

Journal, Golf Range Times, and countless marketing sites online. Alicia has shared the virtual stage with Michael Gerber, Michael Port, Kendall SummerHawk, and many other successful entrepreneurs. Alicia has also appeared as a guest expert on numerous internet radio programs, podcasts, webinars and virtual conferences such as the International Online Business Podcasting Expo.

Alicia is a founding member of the International Association of Coaches, a Certified Teleclass Leader, a Multiple Streams Licensed Coach, a Certified Infinite Possibilities Trainer, a Sixth Sensory Certified Practitioner, and has been the marketing expert for several online forums and membership sites.

In 2006, Alicia authored her bestselling 21 Easy & Essential Steps to Online Success System™. This comprehensive tutorial walks small business owners and entrepreneurs through the process of building a successful and sustainable business online that's guaranteed to bring them to a 6-figure income in half the time they could on their own.

Alicia lives on the eastern seacoast during the school year and at the lake during the summer, with her husband James, daughter Chloe and son Jackson, where she loves her life, both online and off!

YOUR SPECIAL INVITATION...

How would you like to create your own priority-based, highly profitable business in less than part-time hours?

As a reader of *6 Simple Steps to 6 Figures for the Solo Service Professional*, I'd like to invite you into my Mastery of Business Academy Studio Online Coaching Program. If you accept my offer, you'll get immediate access to all the benefits of being a member, and I'll even give you a special gift for investing your time and money in this book.

Just email us at bookoffer@aliciaforest.com and we'll send you the details right away.

I really hope you'll join me and the others who are already enjoying all the benefits of being a part of the MBA Studio!

Cheers,
~ A

Praise from some of Alicia's clients...

"Since working with Alicia I have run two telesminar series, created two info products, doubled my database through a telesummit and filled a live workshop and two high end programs. I made $120,000 in my first twelve months of my new business.

If you want somebody who is there for you when it really counts, when you implement, then Alicia is the right mentor.

Alicia's savvy advice just at the right time helped me to move extremely fast and implement more than I ever could have on my own. I could count on her to be there for me when I needed it the most, in those moments where fear got the better of me. She helped me get clear and get over myself and move forward again.

If you're really serious about building your business, I highly recommend working with Alicia."

Love and Prosperity,
Yvonne McIntosh
Solopreneur Marketing Mentor
Client Prosperity

"I can't say enough about getting the chance to work with Alicia. After attending her Online Business Breakthrough Workshop I signed up on the spot to work with her privately. To kick off our work together I attended a full day private retreat where together we mapped out a plan for my business, my launches, my marketing and how to generate the income I was looking to achieve. Not only did I leave the retreat with exactly what I was looking for but much more. Alicia gives you everything and doesn't hold back. I'm so fortunate to have her as both a mentor and friend and I can't recommend her highly enough. It will be one of the best business decisions you will ever make."

Jeannie Spiro
jeanniespiro.com

"I've attended retreats, both virtual and in-person, with some of the best business coaches out there. And I can honestly say – my time with Alicia was time well-spent and I would do it again in a heartbeat! She was so well-prepared for our in-person retreat, having every aspect of my business mapped out before I had arrived – which allowed us to jump right in! Her business coaching and intuitive guidance was spot-on, and her powerful questions led to many breakthrough moments. And to top it off, her detailed retreat follow-up totally blew me away! She captured every thought, every idea, and every thread of discussion – and gave me even more juicy nuggets to ponder. I have never felt so taken care of in my business!"

Tina Games
journalingbythemoonlight.com

"I've attended all of Alicia's live events (since 2010) and each time I come home with profitable action items. I've worked with Alicia as my coach and trainer and what I love about her is that she gives you all the tools, templates, emails and other resources you need to succeed. She doesn't hold back and she is all about business abundance and wants the same for her clients. Alicia always over delivers and you will be thanking yourself for investing time with her!"

Sandra De Freitas
Author, Does This Blogsite Make My Wallet Look Fat?
wpblogsites.com

"Alicia shifted my thinking profoundly. Because of her coaching, examples, ideas and encouragement, I now have several plans in the works for how I can generate serious money in my business. Before, I had sort of a hazy idea about how to go about it–and I wasn't so confident. Now I am so excited because I feel I have the steps to implement the strategies to make major pay days a reality. After two years of coaching privately with Alicia, I went from zero income to 6-figures, created the brand I'm now known for, held my first live event, and so much more. The bottom line is that Alicia changed my life."

Christine Gallagher
Relationship Marketing Mentor
shesgotclients.com

"Alicia, I wanted to share how coaching with you has enabled me to build a $250,000 business in less than six months and have a team around to support me while I am going through this major ordeal with my family, allowing me the time and energy I need to be present with them. It hasn't been a cake walk, but it is all falling into place and I believe I will break $500K by year end."

Laura Lee Sparks
legalmarketingmaven.com

"Thank you again for your guidance during our half-day & follow-up sessions... I am having an AWESOME summer! I feel so peaceful & relaxed, and I'm having so much FUN with my family -- and just like you said, the momentum in my business & interest in my services has grown substantially!!! THANK YOU, THANK YOU, THANK YOU!!!!"

Dana D'Orsi
danadorsi.com

"For over a year, I had the privilege and the opportunity to have Alicia Forest as my coach. As a result of Alicia's wisdom combined with the structure and support that she has provided, I have made outrageous progress toward setting my foundation for success in my coaching company. I chose a defined target market in the financial services industry and capitalized on my unique personal brand to attract it. I created a valuable signature system and custom designed my website with a free report and opt-in page with Tips to Double Your Income. To further enhance my brand identity, I designed and printed professional marketing collateral. I delivered 9 VIP Days designed to significantly move my clients forward in their businesses. I also created more robust programs including a Diamond, Private Platinum and Gold Level Coaching Programs. I have enrolled my first 2 Private Platinum Clients and a Gold Level client as well. I developed an alliance with another coaching company who will be a strategic partner going forward. During this time, I also generated over $100,000 in new business."

Susan Danzig
Business Development Expert to Financial Services Professionals
susandanzig.com

"I've been in involved with Alicia Forest for a number of years because she is such an amazing and generous woman. I couldn't be happier that I made the decision to attend her Online Business Breakthrough Workshop. I've had so many breakthroughs… I can't even tell you how many I've breakthroughs had! My signature system that I wanted to develop for a number of years has come through very solidly. And I have more confidence than ever that I'll have a very sustainable business for many years to come - forever really, so it's been an honor. If you're thinking about it defiantly go to this event or join one of Alicia's coaching programs."

Anne Deidre
yourintuitivemakeover.com

"I've been following Alicia forest for a few years. I always knew I wanted to work with her at some point and the timing was right now. When I attended her Online Business Breakthrough Workshop, there were definitely lots of breakthroughs. One of the big ones was that I've struggled to create a signature system for years and just by doing the simple technique that we did, I have it really solid and clear. The highlight for me at this event has been the environment that has been created. The support of all the woman that were there, where there's no judgment and I could really be myself and share openly the struggles and successes and get that support and feedback from other people. That was definitely unique to any business type event that I've ever been to. I encourage you to consider attending OBBW or working with Alicia, as I have as a private client. It's the only way to experience what a powerful mentor she is."

Melissa Kitto
communicatewithangels.com

"I've been to a lot of different masterminds, coach environments and to a lot of different events and I have to say that one of the reasons I came to Alicia's event is because I've respected her for a number of years and I really wanted to spend some time with her in person, because what she has created is a business that a lot of us are dreaming of (where she can take the entire summer off), so that really excited me. And what I want to say about OBBW is that Alicia has provided incredibly valuable content. Many of us in the room have had really powerful transformations and she's done it in a way that is so graceful and open-hearted. If you're thinking about doing the Online Business Breakthrough Workshop next year or a working with Alicia, I would highly recommend it. She is one of those heart-centered entrepreneurs who is truly heart-centered."

Amethyst Wyldfyre
theempoweredmessenger.com

"I've been working with Alicia for over two years now and it's hard to summarize how fantastic she is. This is my 2nd workshop that I've been to and I'm amazed at the breakthroughs I'm getting. I'm leaving here with yet another signature system. I also worked with her as a private client last year and just having her in my corner was amazing. She will rock your business world and I highly recommend working with Alicia. She's just awesome."

Donna Ashton
thewaldorfconnection.com

"Alicia, before starting the 21 Steps Program I was an award-winning actress with a one-woman show, a speaker and a forgiveness coach without a plan on how to expand my business by creating an online presence, without any information products to sell and without a clear sense of what steps to take in the right order.

It's just ten weeks, with the direction and focus from you through the live chats and calls, the support and accountability of the group and the additional support of the members of the coaching cafe I hired my first Virtual Assistant to hand off the technical 'stuff' to, created my first information product, held my first two teleseminars, and I'm in the process of setting up my automated systems! Yeah! I've shifted from a sense of confusion and overwhelm into clarity of focus and direction. Now I can reach even more people with my message of forgiveness"

To Your Joy and Freedom,
Brenda Adelman
OUT of Shame, Into Forgiveness, Onward to FREEDOM!!
forgivenessandfreedom

"Alicia, your 10-week program was exactly what I needed to jump-start my action. And talk about RESULTS!!! During the program, I successfully created a new e-course, a new 20 Powerful Minutes Presentation preparation service with accompanying sales page, was interviewed for my first podcast, recorded a podcast myself, created a new brand image for my professional communication consulting work, almost completed a new website, and identified my ideal clients.

I used your suggestions for list-building and I increased my list by more than 100 names in just one month—and that number continues to grow daily. Further, I have more paying clients and people signing up for my paid services regularly now. My cash flow has gone from a trickle to a deluge in just 10 short weeks! I've taken several telecourses with you in the past and each was wonderful for helping me develop a specific part of my business. But what I was missing was a comprehensive plan to pull all the bits and pieces together. Does your program help people succeed? You bet it does! Anyone who follows your simple steps and participates with the support of you and the group will definitely succeed.

Felicia J. Slattery, M.A., M.Ad.Ed.
Communication Consultant, Speaker & Coach
CommunicationTransformation.com

"Working with Alicia in her group progam has been an awesome educational experience! Before I started in the group, I was floundering my way through establishing an online presence for my business. I had some important bits and pieces implemented that I uncovered during my own research. But, I knew I was missing something. I was spending a lot of time trying to implement an online strategy, and I was not confident I was doing it right---which was a HUGE waste of time. I made a choice to shorten my learning curve. That's why I jumped at the chance to sign up for this group!

The program introduced me to a step-by-step approach that helped me complete critical tasks toward establishing an online business. With each step I completed, I felt I was building the strength of my online business. I was extremely motivated knowing others in the group were working on the very same tasks, and I could ask for help when needed. I no longer felt so alone in this online journey!

The most significant improvements I've experienced, so far working with the program, are I learned how to do things that I hadn't even thought about doing before in building an online business… like really fine-tuning who my market niche is, and finding out where they hang out. (It's hard to believe that I was doing this activity all wrong!). Also, Alicia tells what resources are the best ones to use, and how to really find out what my market wants. Best of all, I know I made much greater forward progress by participating in the group, than had I continued to try to do it all on my own.

Through research, I found I was offering my market a product they wanted. But, I was communicating my marketing message wrong! So, I renamed my core product and rolled out a *new and improved* version right away. My subscribers bought and I started earning more money online in no time! I can guarantee you I would not have accomplished this without this group.

In a nutshell, I defined my niche, identified additional niches to market to, created two new for-fee products, a new free taste, I refined my marketing message, and optimized my web site-and I'm not finished, yet! I know exactly how to build my list. I would be thrilled to speak with anyone about this coaching program, and give it my highest recommendation. Thanks, Alicia!"

Bonita L. Richter, MBA
Profit-Strategies.biz

"Alicia's group program has been the perfect 'one-stop shop' for online success. I've been in other programs that give you bits and pieces of the puzzle, but Alicia's program provides the most comprehensive and complete, step-by-step system for building an online business. Prior to participating in Alicia's group, I lacked focus and clarity on the most effective ways to build my online business. Alicia's program was perfect because she guided us along a very logical and methodical path to success. The group interaction and support was an unexpected bonus!

Online success has nothing to do with luck. It requires accountability, support, guidance and specific instruction. Alicia's program gives you all that and more! If you're feeling as overwhelmed as I was when I started out, you've got to take this online program!

Lou Bortone
loubortone.com

"I'm just working through your 21 Easy & Essential Steps to Online Success System program and I wanted to tell you how fantastic I think it is and how much it is helping me - even though I thought I had things very much sussed! I am only on (Step 2) but already I have learned so much more about myself and who I want to work with, I can't wait to make it through to the other side.

I have to tell you, I couldn't put the exercises down (I have them filed in a binder). In the end I had to tell myself to stop as I've got to get the web site written! You've really thought of everything. Many thanks for your time and thanks, again, for your 21 Steps!"

Karen Knowler
TheRawFoodCoach.com

"Prior to participating in the 21 Steps Take Action Group, I was feeling a sense of overwhelm, and a feeling that my business, because it is based on providing professional services, was limited. We all only have 24 hours in a day, so because my business is based on 'selling my time' I was feeling like I didn't have anywhere to 'grow'.

I met Alicia and learned about her 21 Steps program, heard all the wonderful reviews, and I jumped at the opportunity to purchase the program when the revised version came out.

I knew I needed to create passive income streams in order to take my business to the next level and I am a firm believer in investing in your business!

When I heard about the TAG Group, I felt like it was the answer to my next problem; which was 'ok, when do I find the time to read through and implement this program?' I am busy and I sometimes find it difficult to 'schedule' my business development time.

I knew this would be perfect; a weekly set time to be taught the program step by step and an interactive time each week to brainstorm with the group. I love interacting in a group environment, and I was motivated to work through this program, and the group gave me the accountability that was essential.

This has been one of the best investments I have made in my business. By working through the program step by step, I have learned and begun applying list building, product development, and networking steps into my business and I am already seeing the results.

I have also developed great relationships with other professionals in the class and in my opinion those opportunities are always priceless! The weekly chats have been instrumental in helping to clarify and build my ideas for my business. I have picked up two new clients since starting the program (one of them being a member of the class!), launched my blog, created my free taste, and also held my first webinar.

Alicia is a fabulous teacher, and every aspect of this class demonstrates her skills, knowledge, talents and integrity. She gives of herself fully; this is not a 'tease' for something more. This program provides all of the tools and resources you need to begin taking action and creating your passive income streams. It exceeded all of my expectations which in this day and age, is something that I really 'rave' about!

Because of this group I now have the confidence and knowledge to take the ideas that before were just bouncing around inside of my head, and implement the steps to create the passive income my business needs!"

LauraLee Sparks
The Simple Solution Virtual Assistance
TheSimpleSolutionVA.com

"Alicia, I am absolutely on fire!!! Your advice is sound, and the course provided me with practical tools that I can (and will) begin implementing into my business TODAY!!! I am absolutely so excited about what you've shared. I am already thinking of products I can add to my funnel! The great thing is, I KNOW I can follow your program - because like I said, it's practical! I'm not a marketing guru by any means, but this - I can do! THANK YOU SO MUCH for providing such a WONDERFUL course!"

Jenn Givler
jgivlercoaching.com